WHY DID JESUS HAVE TO DIE?

WHY DID JESUS HAVE TO DIE?

AND 20 OTHER QUESTIONS ABOUT JESUS'S
DEATH, RESURRECTION, AND ASCENSION

THE DAILY GRACE CO.®

Contributors

Scott Dickson, Alexa Hess, Suzanne Rhodes,
Jeremy Schmucker, Shelby Turner,
and Spencer Valeri

Editors

Scott Dickson, Jackie Foster, Helen Hummel,
Alli McDougal, and Maren Schettler

Table of Contents

Part II: Jesus's Resurrection

Part III: Jesus's Ascension

The gospel offers hope in the face of death: If you are united to Christ in His death, you can be sure that you will also be raised in Christ.

INTRODUCTION

esus's death, resurrection, and ascension are the most significant milestones in all of human history, and yet His followers have always had questions about these events. Even those who witnessed or experienced these events firsthand often expressed confusion.

As Jesus walked with His disciples throughout Galilee, He told them that He was going to be killed but would rise three days later. The disciples did not understand what He meant, but they were afraid to ask Him their questions (Mark 9:30–32).

After Jesus died and was buried, Mary Magdalene went to His tomb only to find the stone that sealed the tomb rolled away and the linens that wrapped His body lying on the ground. She questioned what had happened to Him, assuming someone had taken His body, and said, "I don't know where they've put him" (John 20:13).

Similarly, Thomas questioned Jesus's bodily resurrection and told his fellow disciples, "If I don't see the mark of the nails in his hands, put my finger into the mark of the nails, and put my hand into his side, I will never believe" (John 20:25).

Finally, as Jesus prepared to ascend back to His Father in heaven, He left His disciples with the truth that though He was leaving, the Spirit would be poured out, and they would be baptized in the Spirit. With their final words to Jesus, they again asked a question: "Lord, are you restoring the kingdom to Israel at this time?" (Acts 1:6).

Like the disciples, you too likely have questions about these events, and that is a good thing. When you ask questions about your Savior and spend time in the Word, you position yourself to be filled by the Spirit, who will lead you to know Christ and the power of His resurrection more deeply (John 15:26). And the more deeply you experience the power of His resurrection, the more fully you can worship Him for who He is and what He has done for you.

As you read through this book, our prayer is that you will experience the love of God displayed for you in Christ's death. Jesus stepped down from heaven, lived a perfect life, and died a sacrificial death for you! He died so that you might be united with Him in His death, and He rose from death to life so that you might be united with Him in His resurrection. One day, you too will die. Yet the gospel offers hope in the face of death: If you are united to Christ in His death, you can be sure that you will also be raised in Christ.

Until that day comes, you will never have all your questions answered, and while you'll never know God completely in this life, you can know Him truly. God promises that if you draw near to Him, He will draw near to you (James 4:8). As you open the pages of this book, we pray that you will not only find answers to your questions but also experience the grace of Jesus and grow in knowledge of who He is (2 Peter 3:18).

Jesus stepped down from heaven, lived a perfect life, and died a sacrificial death for you!

Part I

JESUS'S DEATH

*The One who remained
innocent all throughout His
life took on the most heinous
form of punishment.*

PART I
JESUS'S DEATH

t was something Jesus's disciples thought would never actually occur. Although Jesus told His disciples several times that He was going to die (Matthew 16:21, 17:22–23, 20:17–19), they were probably in denial that this horrible prediction would really take place. But reality likely sank in as they watched their Teacher and Master be arrested and taken away for trial. Then, their greatest fears were realized when Jesus was sentenced to death.

Jesus was severely beaten, spat on, and reviled. He was forced to carry His own heavy cross, and His hands and feet were nailed to the splintered wood. The One who remained innocent all throughout His life took on the most heinous form of punishment meant for the most terrible of criminals: crucifixion.

A crown of thorns, placed upon Jesus's head, dug into His scalp. His clothes were taken away, leaving Him utterly exposed. Above His head hung a mocking sign, which read, "THIS IS THE KING OF THE JEWS" (Luke 23:38). But what the people at Jesus's crucifixion didn't realize was that this sign proclaimed the truth. Jesus was not only the King of the Jews; He was King of all the world. Jesus's accusers didn't crucify a mere man; they crucified the Son of God.

In this section, we will dive deeper into Jesus's death, exploring the reasons why Jesus had to die, what His suffering entailed, and the implications of His death in the lives of believers. We'll also ponder the events that took place during and after Jesus's crucifixion that are often hard to understand. Through it all, we will understand the necessity of Jesus's death more clearly, leading us to greater gratitude for our crucified King.

QUESTION 1

Why did Jesus have to die?

ANSWER:

Because we have sinned, God — being holy, just, and righteous — must punish us with the penalty our sins deserve: death. Only by sending Jesus to die in our place could God spare us from what we deserve.

RELEVANT PASSAGES:

Genesis 2:17
Exodus 34:7
Matthew 26:39
Luke 24:26
John 3:16
Romans 3:25–26, 6:23
Hebrews 9:22–28
1 John 4:10

ow do you show someone that you love them?

Answering that depends on a few factors. For starters, we need to consider the kind of relationship we're talking about. How a husband shows love to his wife will look different in some ways from how he shows love to his friends, which also will differ from the ways he loves his children, his parents, his coworkers, and others. Also, within each of these relationships, there are innumerable ways to show love. For example, spouses may express love differently in happy seasons of life than in difficult ones.

What seems to unite these various expressions of love, though, is one's commitment to another's good, even when that commitment is costly. And this is exactly the type of love described in what is likely the Bible's most famous verse: "For God loved the world in this way: He gave his one and only Son, so that everyone who believes in him will not perish but have eternal life" (John 3:16).

John 3:16 is beloved for good reason. In it, we're given a comforting truth: God loves us. We read of what God in His love provided for us: eternal life. And in between, we see the costly means by which God provided us with this eternal life: the death of His Son, Jesus Christ.

In the span of a few short words, we are told that God has given us an extravagant gift at great cost to Himself.

But did God *have* to do it this way? Was there another means through which He could have given us eternal life? Could John 3:16 have been written differently, saying, "For God loved the world in this [totally different] way . . ."? Or was Jesus's death a necessary requirement for us to experience eternal life?

The first thing we should say in response to that question is that Jesus did not have to die at all. God could have left us to perish in our sins. In His justice, He could have allowed us to experience the full consequences of our actions. In that sense, no, Jesus's death was not necessary. However, given that God chose to offer salvation to sinners, was Jesus's death the only way He could have done so?

Consequent Hypothetical Necessity and Consequent Absolute Necessity

To answer this question, it's important to acknowledge that Scripture is clear that Jesus's death was, in some sense, necessary. Hours before His arrest and crucifixion, Jesus prayed, "My Father, if it is possible, let this cup pass from me" (Matthew 26:39) — the implication being that it was *not* possible for Him to be spared from the cross. And walking with two disciples after His resurrection, Jesus asked them rhetorically, "Wasn't it necessary for the Messiah to suffer these things and enter into his glory?" (Luke 24:26). Both of these statements from Jesus seem to point to the necessity of His crucifixion.

Still, that doesn't fully address the question we're asking. Given that Jesus's death was necessary, *why* was it necessary?

There are two general views regarding this question. The first is sometimes referred to as *consequent hypothetical necessity*. The idea here is that as a *consequence* of God's desire to save sinners, He chose to make the death of Jesus Christ the means by which He would do so, though *hypothetically* He could have chosen another way. Jesus's death, then, was *necessary* simply because God chose that to be the means of salvation. As theologian Robert Letham articulates it, "God, having decreed to save us, could have chosen some other means to do so. However, having chosen this means, it was necessary for our salvation."[1]

In contrast to this, *consequent absolute necessity* claims that God's decision to save sinners required the death of His Son. Letham writes, "This position asserts that, given that God decreed to save his elect, there was no other way he could do this in a manner compatible with his nature than by the death of his Son."[2] In other words, when God chose to save us, He was also choosing to send His Son to die. No other means would achieve the same end.

The Absolute Necessity of Jesus's Death

Faithful Christians can be found advocating for each of these positions, but as we will see, the weight of biblical support seems to favor consequent absolute necessity—the idea that Jesus's death was the only way God could offer us salvation. (Though, as theologian Louis Berkhof acknowledges, this support for consequent absolute necessity is more inferred from Scripture rather than stated outright.[3])

We will briefly consider three reasons for the consequent absolute necessity of Jesus's death.

First, God is holy, just, and righteous and therefore cannot overlook sin. Psalm 5:4 states that "evil cannot dwell with" God, and God Himself says that He "will not leave the guilty unpunished" (Exodus 34:7). Similarly, the Apostle Paul explains that His "wrath is revealed from heaven against all godlessness and unrighteousness" (Romans 1:18). "The important thing," writes Berkhof, is "that the justice of God should be maintained. This clearly points to the fact

---

1   Letham, *Systematic Theology*, 549.
2   Letham, *Systematic Theology*, 551.
3   Berkhof, *Systematic Theology*, combined ed., 370.

that the necessity of the atonement follows from the divine nature."[4] Simply put, a just and holy God *must* respond to sin with punishment.

Important here is Romans 3:26, where Paul says God "presented [Jesus] to demonstrate his righteousness at the present time, so that he would be just and justify the one who has faith in Jesus." This passage shows us, as Berkhof puts it, "that if God were to be righteous and still save people, he had to send Christ to pay the penalty for sins."[5]

Second, the penalty for sin is death. This follows from the previous point. If God must punish sin, then *we* must be punished. Our sin is not a minor defective feature about us; it is "lawlessness" (1 John 3:4), rebellion against our Creator that leaves us under a curse (Galatians 3:10). And Scripture is clear that the penalty for sin is death (Genesis 2:17, Romans 6:23). Payment must be made, and death is that payment.

The sacrificial system God gave to the Israelites communicated this very point. Under the old covenant, the Israelites would bring animals to the tabernacle to be offered to God as a substitute sacrifice; that is, the animal would die in their place. Reflecting on this, Hebrews 9:22 observes that "without the shedding of blood there is no forgiveness." Theologian Michael Horton explains that "blood" in this verse is "shorthand for the whole life of the person that God requires of transgressors."[6]

Another theologian, John Murray, makes an important observation here. He claims that while it's common to think of Jesus's death as following the pattern of Old Testament sacrifices, we ought to do the reverse—think of the Old Testament sacrifices as following the pattern of Jesus's death. As Hebrews 9:23–28 makes clear, the Old Testament sanctuary with its sacrifices was merely a copy of a "true"

---

4   Berkhof, *Systematic Theology*, combined ed., 370.
5   Grudem, *Systematic Theology*, 706–707.
6   Horton, *Pilgrim Theology*, 200.

sanctuary, heaven itself. And so, God's refusal to allow the Israelites to approach the tabernacle without the blood of an animal was designed to illustrate a universal reality: that sinners, who deserve death, cannot approach God unless another dies in their place.

"The necessity of blood-shedding in the Levitical ordinance," Murray writes, "is simply a necessity arising from the necessity of blood-shedding in the higher realm of the heavenly."[7] This strongly supports the idea that Jesus's death was absolutely necessary for our salvation, not merely the option God decided to go with.

Finally, God's love is most clearly demonstrated by the absolute necessity of Jesus's death. Paul writes, "He who did not spare his own Son, but gave him up for us all—how will he not also, along with him, graciously give us all things?" (Romans 8:32, NIV). Paul is highlighting the costliness of what God did for us through Jesus, and it is the "extreme costliness of the sacrifice rendered"—the death of His Son—that makes the cross "the supreme demonstration of the love of God."[8] As the Apostle John writes, "Love consists in this . . . that he loved us and sent his Son to be the atoning sacrifice for our sins" (1 John 4:10).

The Bible views Jesus's death as the ultimate expression of God's love for us—a gift given for our benefit at high cost to Himself. But the cross's ability to display God's intense love for us is lessened when viewed as merely one option among many that God could have used to save us. Nineteenth century theologian A. A. Hodge once spoke quite strongly on this point, writing, "This sacrifice would be most painfully irrelevant if it were anything short of absolutely necessary in relation to the end designed to be attained, that is, unless it be indeed the only possible means to the salvation of sinful man."[9]

---

7   Murray, *Redemption Accomplished and Applied*, 15.
8   Murray, *Redemption Accomplished and Applied*, 17.
9   Hodge, *The Atonement*, 237.

If love brings good to others at a cost to oneself, then no better example of love can be given than Jesus, God's "one and only Son" (John 3:16), who proves God's love by dying for us "while we were still sinners" (Romans 5:8).

Application

Pastor and author Timothy Keller once described the gospel in this way: "We are more sinful and flawed in ourselves than we ever dared believe, yet at the very same time we are more loved and accepted in Jesus Christ than we ever dared hope."[10] We have seen both of these elements in considering the absolute necessity of Jesus's death. The bad news is that we are sinners who deserve nothing from God but His displeasure and wrath. That God should extend His favor to us instead is an act of grace that seems to defy logic.

But that God should extend this favor when the only way to do so came at the cost of His Son—what can we say in response to this? This is an act of love so unprecedented and foreign to our experience that we are often left in stunned silence at the thought of it. It is a beautiful truth that reminds us that the deepest desires of our hearts—to be known, loved, and accepted—are met in Jesus. God could not have done more to demonstrate His love for us than He has by sending His Son to die in our place. We are a loved people. May we always be mindful of this and be comforted by it.

---

10   Keller, *The Meaning of Marriage*, 48.

QUESTION 2

Who was responsible for Jesus's death?

ANSWER:

Many different individuals hold some responsibility for the death of Jesus. This includes the religious leaders of the day, the high priest, the Jews, and Pilate and his Roman soldiers, in addition to all sinners of all time and even God Himself.

RELEVANT PASSAGES:

Matthew 26:3–4, 27:22–37
Mark 15:1
Luke 23:20–25
John 11:47–50, 53, 19:11–12
Acts 2:22–24, 4:27–28
2 Corinthians 5:21

I n the hit film *The Passion of the Christ,*[11] director Mel Gibson makes a cameo appearance. But even if you were looking for him as you watched, you'd never be able to pick him out because his face never appears on screen. All that you see of Gibson is his hand gripped tightly around the nail that's about to be driven through Christ's hand. For Gibson, this was a symbolic moment—a moment reminding him, and all of us, that we are responsible for the death of Christ.

Indeed, rich biblical testimony reminds us that Christ died because of and for our sins. But who is ultimately responsible for His death? By recounting the biblical narrative of His crucifixion, we see many different individuals who bear some responsibility—from the religious leaders and the high priest to the crowds of Jews who gathered and Pontius Pilate and his Roman soldiers. But the responsibility is not only limited to these individuals; we also see the hand of God at work, and—as Gibson so aptly reminds us—we see ourselves. How so? Let's take a look.

---

11   Walls and Pearson, "Gibson Makes Act of Contrition."

The Religious Leaders and the High Priest

Throughout the Gospels, a sort of disdain is directed toward Jesus by the religious leaders of the day (Matthew 21:15; Luke 11:53; John 5:18, 7:45–52). His miracles and teachings regularly angered them and left them accusing Him of blasphemy (Matthew 9:3; Mark 2:6–7; John 8:52–58, 10:31–33). This antagonism climaxes in the assembly of the chief priests and elders, where they conspired to arrest Jesus and have Him killed (Matthew 26:3–4, John 11:47–53).

The plan they hatched apparently involved giving orders that if anyone knew where Jesus was, they should report it so that Jesus could be arrested (John 11:57). Judas complied with this order by leading the servants of the high priest to Jesus to arrest Him (Matthew 26:47, 50).

The council of Jewish leaders (called the Sanhedrin) then looked for false testimony so that they could put Him to death (Matthew 26:59). This sham trial culminated in the high priest, Caiaphas, accusing Jesus of blasphemy, to which the Sanhedrin replied, "He deserves death!" (Matthew 26:65–66). The assembly then gathered together one last time to plot how Jesus could be put to death before they handed Him over to Pilate, the Roman governor of the region (Matthew 27:1–2, Mark 15:1).

In an attempt to seal Jesus's fate and assure the finality of their plan, the chief priests and elders persuaded the crowd to request Jesus's execution, a request which Pilate obliged (Matthew 27:20, 25–26; John 19:12, 16).

Consequently, the evidence against the Sanhedrin is overwhelming. Not only did they plan to arrest and kill Christ, but they also executed their plan with precision. They clearly bear responsibility for the brutal murder of the Son of God.

The Crowds of Jews

The leaders of the Jews, however, are not solely responsible for the death of Christ. The crowds of Jews present at the trial and death of Jesus also bear responsibility. Both Matthew and Luke record that a crowd of Jews cried out to Pilate for Jesus's crucifixion (Matthew 27:22, 25; Luke 23:18–21). Pilate found no guilt in Christ (Luke 23:13–17) and did not want to sentence Him to death, but under pressure from this crowd, Pilate relented and ordered His execution (John 19:12–16).

It may seem like a minor detail in the story of Jesus's death, but the responsibility of the Jews for the death of their own Messiah is not insignificant. After all, they were the ones — of all tribes, tongues, and nations — who were most looking forward to the coming Savior whom God had promised to them. Yet, as Paul would say several decades later in his letter to the Thessalonians, "the Jews . . . killed the Lord Jesus" (1 Thessalonians 2:14–15; see also Acts 2:23). While the Jewish crowds did not actively plot to kill Christ, they failed to recognize Him as the promised Messiah and championed His death, securely placing responsibility for His death on their shoulders.

Pontius Pilate and His Soldiers

The heinousness of this crime isn't attributed only to the Jewish people. The Roman governor, Pontius Pilate, and his soldiers also played a unique role in the death of Christ. Pilate was personally opposed to the execution of Christ, unconvinced of His guilt (Matthew 27:19, 23–24; John 19:6, 12). He made this clear to the crowd by symbolically washing his hands in front of them while saying, "I am innocent of this man's blood" (Matthew 27:24).

Despite his declaration of Jesus's innocence, Pilate certainly bears responsibility for His death because he executed the death sentence (Matthew 27:26–31, Luke 23:24–25, John 19:16). It was at Pilate's command that the Roman soldiers killed Jesus. These soldiers stripped Jesus of His clothes, put a crown of thorns on His head, mocked Him, spat on Him, beat Him with a staff, and crucified Him (Matthew 27:27–37). Later, when Peter preached his sermon on the day of Pentecost, he explained that it was "lawless people" who nailed

Him to the cross and killed Him (Acts 2:23). Surely, those who drove the nails through Jesus's hands are guilty of His death.

God

Interestingly, in the same breath that Peter acknowledged that it was the Romans who executed Christ, he also proclaimed that Jesus "was delivered up according to God's determined plan and foreknowledge" (Acts 2:23). Similarly, while praying for the newly formed Church, Peter and John acknowledged that Herod, Pilate, the Gentiles, and the Jews assembled together against Christ "to do whatever [God's] hand and [his] will had predestined to take place" (Acts 4:27–28; see also John 19:11).

In both of these passages, Peter is declaring that God Himself orchestrated the death of Christ. The events surrounding Jesus's death and even His death itself occurred under the sovereignty of God according to His plan.

When Peter declared that God orchestrated the events that brought about Jesus's death, this was not new theology to the Jews. Centuries prior, Isaiah prophesied about the Messiah's death, declaring that the Lord God "punished him for the iniquity of us all" and was "pleased to crush him severely" (Isaiah 53:6, 10). Similarly, in Revelation, John points to Jesus as "the Lamb who was slaughtered" and indicates that this took place in accordance with God's plan that existed from before "the foundation of the world" (Revelation 13:8; see also 1 Peter 1:18–20). In other words, before God even created the world, He ordained that Jesus would come to die on behalf of His people.

All Sinners — Including Us

Finally, as Mel Gibson so wisely acknowledged, it is because of our sin that Jesus had to die. Sin separates us from God and leads to eternal, spiritual death (Romans 3:23, 6:23). Jesus died as a perfect sacrifice on behalf of His people so that all who put their faith in Him could be reconciled to God. The prophet Isaiah makes this clear: "But he was pierced because of our rebellion, crushed because of our iniquities; punishment for our peace was on him, and we are healed by his wounds" (Isaiah 53:5).

Paul echoes the necessity of Jesus's death on our behalf in Romans 5:6: "For while we were still helpless, at the right time, Christ died for the ungodly."

It is only through the shed blood of Christ that we can be redeemed from the curse of sin (Ephesians 1:7) and reconciled to God (Romans 5:10). So, in a very real sense, it is our sin that made it necessary for Christ to die. We are no better than the chief priests who plotted His arrest, the Jews who demanded His death, or the Roman soldiers who executed Him. We, too, are responsible for the death of Christ.

Application

Jesus died so that sinners could be freed from the penalty and power of sin. If you have placed your faith in Christ by believing in your heart that God raised Him from the dead and if you have confessed with your mouth that Jesus is Lord, then you have been freed from the penalty of sin (Romans 10:9–10). But more than that, you are no longer a slave to the power of sin. You have been united with Christ in the likeness of His death and raised with Him to walk in newness of life. So, while you are responsible for Christ's death, Christ does not hold that against you. He desires you to live a fruitful, Spirit-filled life of obedience.

QUESTION 3

On what day of the week did Jesus die?

_____

ANSWER:

It is widely accepted that Jesus died and was buried on a Friday. However, there are some passages of Scripture that could be interpreted as Jesus dying on Thursday. Whether Jesus died on Thursday or Friday, His death fulfilled the prophecy that He would rise from the dead on the third day, which was Sunday.

RELEVANT PASSAGES:

Hosea 6:2
Matthew 12:39–40, 16:21, 26:17, 27:62, 28:1
Mark 15:42
Luke 9:22, 22:15, 23:54–56
John 19:14, 31
1 Corinthians 15:4

f you look at a calendar to find the date of Easter, you will see that Easter always falls on a Sunday in March or April. You'll also see that Good Friday falls two days before. Good Friday is widely accepted as the day Jesus died and Easter Sunday as the day Jesus rose from the dead. With the day of Jesus's death labeled so clearly on the calendar, one might assume that the issue of what day of the week Jesus died is rather settled. But the truth is that there is some debate about the day Jesus died. And this debate is partly sparked by passages like Matthew 12:40, in which Jesus says that He will "be in the heart of the earth three days and three nights."

Modern logic asserts that if Jesus died on Friday and was prophesied to rise "three days and three nights" after His death, then He would rise from the dead on Monday, as Monday is three days after Friday. But Scripture is clear that Jesus rose from the dead on Sunday. Based on this logic, we come to the conclusion that something isn't lining up—and a slew of questions follow. Did the Gospel writers record the wrong day of resurrection? Did they forget how to count to three? Is the biblical prophecy of Jesus rising on the third day incorrect? Is there something else that we're missing?

Many have searched the timelines of Jesus's death and resurrection as revealed in the Gospels to make sense of this. From this search, there have emerged two main views on which day Jesus died. The most widely accepted view is that Jesus died on Friday and that He was dead not for three full days but for at least a part of three separate days. Another viable view is that Jesus died on Thursday, making His Sunday resurrection three full days after His death.

Let's take a look at both views, but first, let's remind ourselves of the timeline of the last few days of Jesus's life and the day of His

CHART 1

Jesus and His disciples gather for the Passover meal (also known as the Last Supper).	Matthew 26:17–29 • Mark 14:12–25 Luke 22:7–23 • John 13:1–20
Jesus prays in the garden of Gethsemane.	Matthew 26:36–46 • Mark 14:32–42 Luke 22:39–46 • John 18:1
Judas betrays Jesus, and Jesus is arrested.	Matthew 26:47–56 • Mark 14:43–50 Luke 22:47–53 • John 18:2–11
Jesus comes before the high priest (Caiaphas) and the council.	Matthew 26:57–68 • Mark 14:53–65 Luke 22:66–71 • John 18:12–14, 19–24
Jesus comes before Pilate.	Matthew 27:1–2, 11–26 • Mark 15:1–15 Luke 23:1–25 • John 18:28–40
Jesus is mocked, beaten, and placed on the cross.	Matthew 26:67–68, 27:27–44 Mark 14:65–67, 15:16–32 Luke 22:63–65, 23:26–43 John 18:22–23, 19:1–27
Jesus dies.	Matthew 27:45–56 • Mark 15:33–41 Luke 23:44–49 • John 19:28–37
Jesus is buried.	Matthew 27:57–61 • Mark 15:42–47 Luke 23:50–56 • John 19:38–42
The Sabbath takes place.	Matthew 28:1 • Mark 15:42, 16:1 Luke 23:56 • John 19:42
Jesus rises from the dead.	Matthew 28:1–10 • Mark 16:1–8 Luke 24:1–12 • John 20:1–10

resurrection. Once we have this timeline laid out in our mind's eye, we'll be able to better understand these two theories about the day Jesus died.

The Timeline of Jesus's Death and Resurrection

Chart 1 details the events of Jesus's death and resurrection between the Last Supper and Resurrection Day, including Scripture references. Chart 2 shows on which days these events would have fallen if Jesus died on a Friday.

CHART 2

Jesus and His disciples gather for the Passover meal (also known as the Last Supper).	Thursday
Jesus prays in the garden of Gethsemane.	Thursday
Judas betrays Jesus, and Jesus is arrested.	Thursday
Jesus comes before the high priest (Caiaphas) and the council.	Thursday
Jesus comes before Pilate.	Friday
Jesus is mocked, beaten, and placed on the cross.	Friday
Jesus dies.	Friday
Jesus is buried.	Friday
The Sabbath takes place.	Saturday
Jesus rises from the dead.	Sunday

Chart 3 shows on which days these events would have fallen if Jesus died on a Thursday.

CHART 3

Jesus and His disciples gather for the Passover meal (also known as the Last Supper).	Wednesday
Jesus prays in the garden of Gethsemane.	Wednesday
Judas betrays Jesus, and Jesus is arrested.	Wednesday
Jesus comes before the high priest (Caiaphas) and the council.	Wednesday
Jesus comes before Pilate.	Thursday
Jesus is mocked, beaten, and placed on the cross.	Thursday
Jesus dies.	Thursday
Jesus is buried.	Thursday
The Sabbath takes place.	Saturday
Jesus rises from the dead.	Sunday

Evidence Jesus Died on Friday

For millennia, the most widely accepted day of Jesus's death has been Friday, and there are several reasons why. The main two reasons are the contextual information given in Scripture about each day leading up to Jesus's death and the Jewish understanding of a day.

First, let's walk through the contextual information given in Scripture that leads us to believe that Jesus died on a Friday. The most convincing contextual information centers on where the Sabbath falls in the timeline of Jesus's death and resurrection. The Sabbath is mentioned in all four Gospels, and all four point out that Jesus died the day before the Sabbath and was quickly buried before the

Sabbath began. The Sabbath began at sundown on Friday and ended at sundown on Saturday. Thus when Mark 15:42, Luke 23:56, and John 19:42 say Jesus's family and followers rested on the Sabbath after they buried Him in the tomb, we can infer that they buried Him on Friday and He was in the tomb on Saturday. And when Matthew 28:1, Luke 24:1, and John 20:1 say that Jesus's resurrection took place on the first day of the week, which was Sunday, the day after the Sabbath—we're led to the same conclusion.

Yet there is still a problem. If Jesus died on a Friday and rose on a Sunday, how could He have been raised on the third day? How can Sunday be three days after Friday? This is when it's important to understand the Jewish understanding of a day. This understanding has two parts. First, unlike the modern world, Jewish days did not begin in the morning but at sundown. In other words, new days didn't dawn with the rising sun for first-century Jews; they began as the horizon darkened and the sun left sight. Therefore, if Jesus was crucified and died before sundown Friday, which is what all of the Gospel accounts record, then Jesus was dead on Friday—day one. He was dead on Saturday, the Sabbath—day two. And He rose again on the third day, Sunday—day three. It's entirely possible and even probable, based on contextual information and the Jewish understanding of a day, that Jesus died on Friday.

Evidence Jesus Died on Thursday

However probable it is that Jesus died on Friday, another viable option is that He died on Thursday. The week of Jesus's death was a significant one for the Jewish people; it was the week of Passover. During Passover, the Jewish people gathered with friends and family to eat a meal that commemorated God's deliverance of His people from Egypt. The Passover meal was typically eaten on Friday. (However, Passover was often celebrated over the course of a week, and the meal could, at times, be enjoyed on a day other than Friday—which explains why Jesus and His disciples may have eaten it on Thursday if He did, in fact, die on Friday.)

The Passover meal is referenced a few times in the Gospel accounts of Jesus's final days. One of these references is significant in the argument that Jesus died on Thursday. John 19:31 says that while Jesus was on the cross, it was the preparation day for a special Sabbath day. To Jews in the first-century world—and even today—the Sabbath was a day of rest observed on Saturdays. Yet the word "Sabbath" is not only used in this context; the Passover has also historically been called a *special* Sabbath day because it was a special day that occurred before the Sabbath. Thus during the week of Passover, there were two days that could have been referred to as a Sabbath—the "normal" Sabbath (which occurred on Saturday) and the "special" Sabbath (which occurred on Friday).

If the Sabbath described in John 19:31 was meant to refer to the special Sabbath day (i.e., Friday) rather than the normal Sabbath day (i.e., Saturday), then it would make sense that Jesus died and was buried on Thursday. At the same time, the other Gospels don't seem to support a Thursday death as clearly as John.

Application

The Bible doesn't conclusively say on which day of the week Jesus died, but it does clearly say why Jesus died. He died so that our sins might be forgiven and we might have life in Him. It's important to have an understanding of when Jesus died so that we can see that the Bible does not contradict itself and so that we can defend the unity and perfection of Scripture. But more important than the date Jesus died is what His death accomplished. We do not need to know the day of His death to receive the salvation He offers as the resurrected Savior. Scripture is not definitive on everything, but it is definitive on the most important things.

QUESTION 4

What was Jesus's suffering on the cross like?

_____

ANSWER:

On the cross, Jesus suffered in order to pay the penalty for our sins. This suffering included enduring physical pain, bearing our sins, being abandoned by God, and experiencing the wrath of God.

RELEVANT PASSAGES:

Isaiah 51:22, 53:4–12
Matthew 26:39, 27:28–30, 46
Mark 14:34
John 1:29, 19:1–3
Romans 3:25–26
Galatians 3:13
2 Corinthians 5:21
Hebrews 9:28
1 Peter 2:24
1 John 2:2

ne of the most important concepts related to Christ's death is that of the atonement. But for many of us, "atonement" is not a word we use every day. So, what does it mean, and what does it have to do with Jesus's suffering? We will cover the significance of the atonement more in Question 10, but for now, we can benefit from evangelical theologian Wayne Grudem's definition: "the work Christ did in his life and death to earn our salvation."[12] = atonement

There are two broad aspects of Christ's work during His life and death that brought us salvation. These are often referred to as Christ's active and passive obedience.

When we speak about Christ's active obedience, we primarily have in mind that Christ perfectly obeyed the requirements of the Law and the will of the Father. He "did not know sin" during His life (2 Corinthians 5:21), and He upheld every Old Testament law. Through His perfect life, Christ earned righteousness for us (Romans 5:19), and His blemish-free life qualified Him to die as a perfect sacrifice for sin (1 Peter 1:19, 2:22; Hebrews 9:14).

---

12   Grudem, *Systematic Theology*, 705.

On the other hand, the suffering of Christ's life, including His death, is referred to as His passive obedience. He suffered and died on the cross, offering Himself as a sacrifice for sin and paying its penalty.

As we tackle the question, "What was Jesus's suffering on the cross like?" we are thinking about Christ's passive obedience, but it's important to know that Christ's passive obedience was not restricted to His suffering leading up to and including His crucifixion. Christ's entire life involved suffering. In fact, the book of Hebrews says, "Although he was the Son, he learned obedience from what he suffered" (Hebrews 5:8). Throughout His life, Jesus suffered in many different ways — for example, He suffered the attacks of Satan during His temptation (Matthew 4:1–11), He suffered opposition from the Jewish leaders during His ministry (Hebrews 12:3–4), and because He was God in the flesh, He saw the brokenness of humanity in a unique way. We can only imagine how troubled this left His soul. This is likely why the prophet Isaiah calls Him "a man of sorrows and acquainted with grief" (Isaiah 53:3, ESV).

Jesus's grief seems to reach a climax as He nears His crucifixion. In the garden of Gethsemane, He tells Peter, James, and John, "I am deeply grieved to the point of death," and then He prays, "My Father, if it is possible, let this cup pass from me" (Matthew 26:38–39). In this moment, Jesus is anticipating the suffering He will experience during His crucifixion. This suffering can be thought of in four different aspects: enduring physical pain, bearing sin, being abandoned by God, and experiencing the wrath of God. Let's take a look at each.

Enduring Physical Pain

Scripture is quite clear that Jesus endured an immense amount of physical pain. The Gospels record that prior to being nailed to the cross, Jesus was flogged and beaten with a staff (Mark 14:65, 15:15–19). The Bible, though, does not give many details about the physical nature of Christ's crucifixion other than to say He was crucified and that nails were driven through each of His hands and His feet (Luke 24:39–40; John 20:20, 25, 27; Acts 2:23).

However, while the Bible lacks explicit details about the nature of Christ's crucifixion, history attests that crucifixion "is arguably the most brutal, shameful, and inhuman death penalty to ever enter the mind of humankind." Josephus, a first-century Jewish historian, referred to it as the "most wretched of deaths,"[13] and Cicero, a Roman statesman, called it the "worst extreme of the tortures inflicted upon slaves."[14]

Crucifixion killed criminals by eventually suffocating them. In order to breathe well, the crucified man had to lift his body with his legs, but this put extreme pressure on the nails through his ankles and also flexed his arms, which caused searing pain in both his arms and legs. This agony would sometimes be drawn out for days as he awaited suffocation (John 19:31–33).[15] To many of us, this type of physical pain is unimaginable; yet, while agonizing for Christ, His other sufferings on the cross may have been harder to bear.

Bearing Sin

Christ was Immanuel, God with us — the image of the invisible God (Matthew 1:23, Colossians 1:15). This means that Christ was perfectly holy. He was absolutely separate from sin and all kinds of evil. Sin is the antithesis of all that Christ is, and He hates it. Yet in those moments on the cross, Scripture says that He took on Himself all of the sins of His people (1 Peter 2:24). Suddenly, all that He hated was put upon Him.

Scripture uses several different phrases to describe Christ's act of taking our sins upon Himself. Isaiah 53:6 (ESV) says, "the LORD has *laid on him* the iniquity of us all," and then later, Isaiah 53:12 says, "he *bore* the sin of many." In the New Testament, Peter also writes,

---

13 Bass, *The Bedrock of Christianity*, 92.

14 Bass, *The Bedrock of Christianity*, 92.

15 Grudem, *Systematic Theology*, 572–573.

"He himself *bore our sins* in his body on the tree" (1 Peter 2:24). The anonymous author of Hebrews similarly writes that He was "offered once to *bear* the sins of many" (Hebrews 9:28). Paul writes that Christ was made "*to be* sin" (2 Corinthians 5:21) and that He redeemed us by "*becoming* a curse for us" (Galatians 3:13). Each of these verbs (which we have emphasized via italics) communicate the idea that Christ took our sins upon Himself. We can only imagine the inner turmoil and suffering Christ must have felt as He bore the guilt for our sin.

Being Abandoned by God

Christ's anguish and suffering under the guilt of sin were further amplified, because on the cross, for the first time, He was separated from the Father. Since eternity past, Jesus—the Son of God—and God the Father have always enjoyed intimate fellowship (John 17:5, 21). But now, in these moments of extreme suffering under the guilt of many, Jesus was not experiencing the love of His Father (John 17:26), which caused Him to cry out, "My God, my God, why have you abandoned me?" (Matthew 27:46).

Experiencing the Wrath of God

But perhaps even worse than being abandoned by the Father was the pain Jesus experienced by bearing the wrath of God. Scripture teaches that the wrath of God comes upon sinners (Romans 1:18, John 3:36, Ephesians 5:6). So, when Jesus took the guilt of sin upon Himself, He experienced the wrath of God that is reserved for sinners (John 3:35–36, Matthew 26:39; see also Psalm 75:8, Isaiah 51:22, Jeremiah 25:15).

In some English translations of the New Testament (such as the NASB or ESV), this is described as the act of making propitiation for sins (Romans 3:25–26; Hebrews 2:17; 1 John 2:2, 4:10, NASB). To "propitiate" simply means "to regain favor,"[16] and in its New Testament

---

16   Merriam-Webster, "propitiate."

context, the word "propitiation" means "averting the wrath of God by the offering of a gift."[17] By bearing the guilt of sin, Christ also bore the wrath of God, and in doing so, He turned away the wrath of God from us and made Him favorable toward us.[18]

Therefore, it is now possible for us to be spared from the horrible reality of experiencing the wrath of God (Romans 5:9, 1 Thessalonians 5:9). Praise God! For it is indeed a "terrifying thing to fall into the hands of the living God" (Hebrews 10:31).

Christ's experience on the cross was agonizing and full of despair. He suffered not only physical pain and death but also the psychological pain of bearing sin, being abandoned by His Father, and experiencing God's wrath. Yet He endured to the point of death, knowing that He came "to give his life as a ransom for many" (Mark 10:45). The author of Hebrews sums up this purpose: "[Christ] has appeared one time, at the end of the ages, for the removal of sin by the sacrifice of himself" (Hebrews 9:26).

Application

Second Corinthians 5:21 simply and succinctly summarizes many of the truths we've discussed so far: "He made the one who did not know sin to be sin for us, so that in him we might become the righteousness of God." God the Father put our sins on Christ. In other words, "He thought of them as belonging to Christ."[19] This means that God sees the guilt for our sins as "belonging to Christ rather than to us."[20]

Have you ever thought deeply about what this truth means for you? It means that if you have placed your faith in Christ, then you are the righteousness of God. He does not view you with disdain. He

---

17 Duncan, "Propitiation."

18 Grudem, *Systematic Theology*, 713.

19 Grudem, *Systematic Theology*, 575.

20 Grudem, *Systematic Theology*, 575.

is not waiting to pour out His wrath on you. You are the object of His grace in Christ, and He sees you as holy and righteous. You have been reconciled to the Father, freed from your bondage to sin, and invited to live a life for His glory.

QUESTION 5

What can we learn from Jesus's final recorded words?

ANSWER:

Jesus spoke these words to confirm that He accomplished God's plan for salvation through His death on the cross. As He finished this work, Jesus entrusted His spirit to the Lord, confident that God would deliver Him from death.

RELEVANT PASSAGES:
Matthew 27:50–51
Mark 15:37–38
Luke 12:50, 18:31, 23:46
John 4:34, 17:4, 19:30

If you knew you were going to die, what would you want to say to those around you in your final moments? Perhaps you would express your love for your family or say something inspirational and moving, something that would be remembered.

The words spoken by Jesus as He hung dying on the cross carry eternal significance for their hearers, both then and now. In Luke and John, we see two of the statements Jesus made in His final moments on the cross: "Father, into your hands I entrust my spirit" (Luke 23:46), and "It is finished" (John 19:30).

These words have tremendous impact, as they reveal Christ's trust in the Father and His completion of the work that God sent Him to accomplish. Let's take a look at both of these statements to see what we can learn from each.

"Father, into your hands I entrust my spirit."

When Jesus cried out, "Father, into your hands I entrust my spirit" (Luke 23:46), He was quoting Psalm 31:5, which says, "Into your hand I entrust my spirit; you have redeemed me, LORD, God of truth."

Psalm 31 was written by David as he was experiencing affliction from his enemies. Rather than despair, he sought protection in the

Lord and entrusted his life to Him. His hope and trust in God's deliverance can be seen in Psalm 31:4, which reads, "You will free me from the net that is secretly set for me, for you are my refuge." Jesus's recitation of Psalm 31:5 reflects a similar trust in God's deliverance. Even as Jesus was dying on the cross, He trusted in God's plan and hoped in God's deliverance. Jesus trusted that death was not the end for Him.

Jesus's words also demonstrated His relationship with God. Jesus calls God "Father" in the verse, which describes His intimate relationship with God—a Trinitarian relationship. Jesus is the Son, and God is the Father—and as the Son, Jesus remained completely obedient to His Father all the way up to His death (Philippians 2:8).

Jesus was also entirely aligned with the Father's will. Jesus did not resist God's will for Him to give up His life; He humbly yielded to the Father. And as He gave up His spirit on the cross, He entrusted His spirit to the Father, knowing that just as God was faithful to fulfill His plan through Him, so would God be faithful to deliver Him from death.

"It is finished."

When we turn to the Gospel of John, we see another phrase Jesus uttered in His final moments on the cross: "It is finished" (John 19:30). Just as Jesus's statement in Luke 23:46 demonstrated His obedience to God, so do His words in John 19:30.

Jesus spoke throughout His ministry about the "work" that God had for Him on earth. For example, in John 4:34, Jesus said, "My food is to do the will of him who sent me and to finish his work." In Luke 12:50, Jesus referred to the work He was called to accomplish as His "baptism," saying, "But I have a baptism to undergo, and how it consumes me until it is finished!"

Later, when Jesus was in Gethsemane, praying before His imminent arrest and death, Jesus declared to God, "I have glorified you on the earth by completing the work you gave me to do" (John 17:4). Though Jesus had not yet gone to the cross, Jesus had been obedient to God's plan up to that point. He faithfully taught truths about God's kingdom, glorified God, healed the sick and hurting, and devoted years to a group of twelve disciples. What work, then, was left for Jesus to accomplish?

In addition to coming to earth and living the perfect life, Jesus's death on the cross accomplished God's plan to save and redeem His people from sin. In John 19:28, John describes Jesus's final moments on the cross: "After this, when Jesus knew that everything was now finished that the Scripture might be fulfilled, he said, 'I'm thirsty.'" John's words show us Jesus's awareness that His death was accomplishing God's plan of salvation. He knew that the Scriptures that prophesied about His death and promised redemption were now fulfilled in and through His sacrifice. And so, in His final moments, Jesus cried, "It is finished" (John 19:30).

While Jesus's words on the cross declare that He had finished all God had asked Him to accomplish, the final work of restoration is yet to be complete. If we are in Christ, we have been made new and reconciled in our relationship with God. But we, as well as all creation, currently await total restoration (Revelation 21), when Jesus will return to set all things right. God's Word assures us: This restoration that we long for will one day be complete.

In Revelation 21, John witnesses a vision of what the new heaven and new earth will look like. He sees this broken world restored to a world without sin or pain. As he witnesses this vision, he hears these words come from God's throne: "It is done! I am the Alpha and the Omega, the beginning and the end" (Revelation 21:6). Jesus's words on the cross point forward to the words He will one day speak when all of creation is restored. Yes, His work was finished on the cross, but it will be fully and finally complete when He returns to bring about restoration.

Application

Because the work of salvation was finished on the cross, there is nothing additional we need to do in order to be saved from our sin. There is no need for us to do any work, for Christ has done all the work on our behalf. All that is required of us is to put our faith in Christ's work, believing that it is because of His death on the cross that we are saved.

As we continue to live in the pain and grief of life, awaiting the complete fulfillment of God's plan of redemption and restoration, we can do so with trust in the Lord. Like Jesus, we can entrust ourselves to God, knowing He has already delivered us from sin and one day will deliver us from this broken world. Until then, we trust in Him and look ahead to eternity with hope.

QUESTION 6

How are the physical events that coincided with Christ's death significant?

ANSWER:

The temple curtain split, signifying the access to God we now have through Christ, and the earth darkened, signifying the judgment Jesus took on for our sin.

RELEVANT PASSAGES:

Matthew 27:45, 50–51
Mark 15:33, 37–38
Luke 23:44–45

here are times in our lives when a physical occurrence serves to signal that something important is happening. Gray clouds rolling in on a sunny day indicate that a storm is brewing. The piercing alarm of a police car means that there's trouble—an accident or crime, perhaps. The blow of a lifeguard's whistle and their frantic gestures reveal that there is danger in the water. Likewise, there are two physical events that take place during Christ's crucifixion and point to a deeper truth. These events speak to the mighty work that Jesus was accomplishing on the cross, signifying the judgment Jesus was taking on for our sins and the access to God that He made possible for us.

The Earth Darkening

As Jesus hung on the cross, darkness descended on the earth. This darkness wasn't due to the time of day—it was only noon. It wasn't caused by a turn in the weather. A storm was not brewing, for there were no claps of lightning, raging winds, or rushing rain. This darkness wasn't a natural phenomenon either. Some have suggested that a solar eclipse must have been occurring. But Jesus's crucifixion took place during Passover, and Passover occurred during a full moon.[21] Because a

---

21   Schnabel, *Mark*, 419.

solar eclipse can only happen during a new moon, it is not scientifically possible that this darkness was caused by an eclipse. If not any of these theories, then what was happening?

The darkness was a God-ordained event meant to communicate God's judgment that Jesus was experiencing on the cross. The Bible often associates darkness with God's judgment. For example, the ninth plague God brought upon Egypt was darkness (Exodus 10:21–23), and it was during the night that God brought about the tenth and final plague, the killing of every firstborn son (Exodus 12:12–13).

Similarly, the prophets pick up this imagery of darkness, equating it with God's judgment. In Amos 8:9, the prophet Amos prophesies, "And in that day—this is the declaration of the Lord God—I will make the sun go down at noon; I will darken the land in the daytime." Similarly, Zephaniah writes, "That day is a day of wrath, a day of trouble and distress, a day of destruction and desolation, a day of darkness and gloom, a day of clouds and total darkness" (Zephaniah 1:15). This darkness signifies the judgment evildoers would experience from the Lord, as He poured out His wrath upon them.

Therefore, the darkness that God brought upon the land at Jesus's death signified His wrath being poured out on Jesus for our sin. The land was literally made dark, but the darkness was also spiritual, as it demonstrated how Jesus was taking God's wrath upon Himself, being punished in our place. The darkness of Jesus's death would soon be replaced with the light of His resurrection. But in these moments on the cross, the heavy darkness that remained for three hours indicated to all those who witnessed Jesus's crucifixion that the Father was pouring out judgment on the Son.

The Temple Curtain Splitting

The darkness was not the only physical event that took place while Jesus was on the cross. Right after Jesus took His last breath, an earthquake occurred, and the temple curtain was torn in two from the top to the bottom (Matthew 27:51), demonstrating that the way into God's presence was now open and available for all.

When the high priest would go into the Most Holy Place (the innermost sanctuary of the temple, set apart for God's presence to dwell), he would bring the blood of a sacrifice to atone for the people's sins. With the people's sins atoned, or covered, the people were temporarily restored to a right relationship with God. But the priest would have to make the sacrifice year after year in order to continually cover the people's sins.

Jesus, however, "appeared one time, at the end of the ages, for the removal of sin by the sacrifice of himself" (Hebrews 9:26b). Jesus's sacrifice is sufficient, which means that the atonement we receive through His salvation covers our sins completely and permanently. With all of our sins atoned for, we are able to be in a right relationship with God. Our sin no longer separates us from Him. Just as the torn curtain provided access to the Most Holy Place, so does Jesus provide us access to God.

God ordained both of these natural events—the darkness and the earthquake that caused the temple curtain to tear. God's choice for these events to happen teaches us that God wanted people to truly see what He was accomplishing through Christ, displaying His power and inviting them to believe in His redemption.

Application

God is faithful to fulfill His promises and plans, and the events at the time of Jesus's death attest to that truth. Because God has fulfilled His plan of redemption by pouring out His judgment upon Christ, we live in freedom and have peace with God (Romans 5:1, Galatians 5:1). We also have access to God and delight in His presence that is always with us. These blessings motivate us to live in gratitude for the judgment Jesus took on for our sake and to embrace our access to God by coming to Him in prayer. As we walk in Christ's freedom and delight in God's presence, we are encouraged to trust God's ways and plans. Just as God was intentional with every detail at Christ's death, so will He intentionally care for every detail of our lives. We can trust God's faithfulness to us, confident that nothing escapes His notice or is beyond His control.

QUESTION 7

Who were the people raised
to life after Jesus's death?

_____

ANSWER:

The people raised to life after Jesus's death were believers who died prior to Jesus's sacrificial death. They received glorified bodies as a preview of the glorification that we will experience when Christ returns.

RELEVANT PASSAGE:
Matthew 27:52–53

ave you ever been watching the news or reading an article only to encounter an interesting tidbit mentioned in passing? Suddenly, you find yourself curious and going down a rabbit trail, trying to learn more about that seemingly random piece of information. In his account of Jesus's death, Matthew makes a brief statement about some saints being resurrected and appearing to many people in Jerusalem. He writes: "The tombs were also opened and many bodies of the saints who had fallen asleep were raised. And they came out of the tombs after his resurrection, entered the holy city, and appeared to many" (Matthew 27:52–53).

This short snippet concludes a list of events that coincided with the death of Christ, and it prompts the curiosity of many readers. Who were these people who were raised from the dead? What was the nature of this resurrection? Why were they resurrected?

In this chapter, we are going to attempt to provide as much clarity as possible around this event. To do so, we will think through this narrative according to the Five Ws of journalism: who, what, when, where, and why.

Who?

Who exactly were these folks who came back to life? Unfortunately, Matthew doesn't specifically identify them, but he does give a few details about them.

First, he identifies them as "saints." The Greek word used here is *hagios*,[22] which means "holy" or "set apart." When used in the context of people, it typically refers to believers who have been set apart for God's purposes. Matthew is telling us that these are believers who died prior to Jesus's death.

Second, he describes them as "many bodies of the saints." This gives us an indication as to the number of saints. It wasn't that all old covenant believers were raised but rather a select amount.

Finally, we learn that these saints are those "who had fallen asleep." The phrase "fallen asleep" was commonly used in Greco-Roman culture as a metaphor for death. Both Luke and Paul use it in their canonical writings (Acts 7:60; 1 Corinthians 15:6, 51; 1 Thessalonians 4:13). Therefore, those who "were raised" and brought back to life were believers who had died prior to Christ's death. Some scholars hypothesize that they were the patriarchs of the faith or other well-known individuals, and others suggest they were saints who had recently died because their bodies were still in the tombs. However, given the lack of detail, it seems unwise to insist on an identity more specific than that of believers who died before Jesus did.

What?

Many of the questions that surround this brief statement from Matthew center on the nature of the event. What kind of resurrection was this? Was this a resurrection by which the saints were raised to natural bodies, like that of Lazarus (John 11)? Or were these saints given glorified bodies, never to die again (1 Corinthians 15:35–49)?

---

22   Aland et al., *Greek New Testament*, 112.

It's tough to be certain because Matthew doesn't give us any details upon which to build an argument.

However, if the purpose of Matthew's comment is to demonstrate the significance of Christ's death and resurrection, it seems likely that this was a resurrection to glorified bodies. Through His death and resurrection, Christ has accomplished the resurrection of these saints, which serves as a guarantee of our own glorious resurrection at Christ's coming.

When and Where?

Jesus's death was immediately followed by the tearing of the sanctuary curtain and an earthquake. This earthquake split rocks apart and opened the tombs (Matthew 27:50–51). The location of these tombs is not specifically identified, though they were probably in a Jewish cemetery outside the city of Jerusalem. What happened next is debated by scholars. Did the saints immediately rise from the dead when the tombs were opened by the earthquake? And if so, did they just stay near their tombs for three days until Jesus's own resurrection, at which point they entered the city and began appearing to others? Or did they rise from the dead after Jesus's own resurrection, in which case they rose from the dead and immediately came out of the tombs?[23]

Scholars who hold the latter view usually do so in an attempt to reconcile this passage with 1 Corinthians 15:20, which says Jesus has been appointed to be "the firstfruits of those who have fallen asleep" (see also Acts 26:23). These scholars insist that it hardly makes sense for a resurrection of some saints to occur before Jesus if He is the "firstfruits" of those resurrected, being that He is the guarantee of further resurrections.

However, it does not seem necessary to insist on such an interpretation. Scholars who hold to the former position believe that

---

23   Johnson, "Matthew 27:51–54 Revisited."

1 Corinthians 15:20 is speaking specifically to the yet-future resurrection of all believers at the time of Christ's return. Since Paul has the future resurrection in mind when he makes that statement about Christ, the fact that a select number of saints have already been resurrected may not be relevant. Christ's resurrection is still a guarantee for all those who have yet to experience resurrection.

Regardless of which position we might hold, we can agree that this select group of saints who experienced resurrection at the moment of Christ's death were as a sign pointing to the importance of His death.[24] The appearance of these saints in resurrected bodies to many in Jerusalem is a testament to Christ's own resurrection and a preview of our own.

Why?

The details surrounding this account are surprisingly sparse, and perhaps Matthew did that on purpose to draw attention to the few words that he did use. Twice in this short account, he uses the word *hagios*[25] (translated as "saints" and "holy city") to stress the meaning of the events. Previously, Matthew had presented Jerusalem as the city that "kills the prophets" (Matthew 23:37) and killed the Messiah. But in anticipation of its future re-creation (Revelation 21:2, 10), which is guaranteed by the death and resurrection of Christ, Matthew here calls it "the holy city."

The resurrection of these saints and their appearance to many in the holy city serve to remind us that by giving up His own life, Christ gave eternal life to others. His death guarantees that those who believe in Him will themselves be delivered from death and resurrected to eternal life in eternal bodies in His eternal kingdom. Scholar Craig Keener summarizes the purpose of this brief section by saying,

---

24   Hendricksen, *New Testament Commentary: Matthew*, 976.

25   Aland et al., *Greek New Testament*, 112.

"The raising of dead persons at Jesus's death reminds us that by refusing to save himself, Jesus did save others."[26]

Application

As believers in Christ, we do not have to fear death, for when we die, we go immediately to be with the Lord in His heavenly kingdom (John 14:3, 2 Corinthians 5:6–8, Philippians 1:23). We also have hope that one day He will return and eternally join us with our own resurrected bodies (John 5:25–29; Romans 8:23, 30; 1 Thessalonians 4:15–17). The hope of a secure future with Jesus and without pain and suffering should give us great confidence to face today. We can boldly serve Jesus Christ without fear or reservation because the power of death has been broken (1 Corinthians 15:54–55).

Paul gives us a great application of the truth of our future resurrection in 1 Corinthians 15:57–58: "But thanks be to God, who gives us the victory through our Lord Jesus Christ! Therefore, my dear brothers and sisters, be steadfast, immovable, always excelling in the Lord's work, because you know that your labor in the Lord is not in vain."

The truth of a future resurrection should motivate us to work heartily for the Lord. We can serve Him steadfastly, knowing that death has been swallowed up in victory and that victory belongs to those in Christ, who will one day experience resurrection to everlasting life.

---

26   Keener, *Matthew*, 390.

QUESTION 8

Did Jesus go to hell when He died?

ANSWER:

When Jesus died, He did not descend into hell; rather, His spirit went to be with His Father in heaven, and His body was buried.

RELEVANT PASSAGES:

Acts 2:27
Romans 10:6–7
Ephesians 4:8–9
1 Peter 3:18–20, 4:6

The Apostles' Creed

I believe in God, the Father Almighty,
Maker of heaven and earth.
and in Jesus Christ, his only Son, our Lord;
Who was conceived of the Holy Spirit,
born of the Virgin Mary,
suffered under Pontius Pilate,
was crucified, dead, and buried.
He descended into hell.[27]
The third day he rose again from the dead.
He ascended into heaven
and sits at the right hand of God the Father Almighty,
whence He shall come to judge the quick and the dead.
I believe in the Holy Spirit,
the holy catholic[28] *Church,*
the communion of saints,
the forgiveness of sins,
the resurrection of the body,
and the life everlasting.
Amen.[29]

---

27 Some versions omit this line altogether, and others say, "He descended to the dead."

28 The word "catholic" that is used here means "universal" and refers to all believers. It is not a reference to the Roman Catholic Church.

29 Mohler, *The Apostles' Creed*, xi.

he Apostles' Creed famously states that Christ "was crucified, dead, and buried. He descended into hell." This statement has led Christians over the years to believe that Jesus went to hell when He died. But do the Scriptures teach that?

Before diving into the pages of the Bible to answer this question, let's look closer at the development of the phrase "He descended into hell." The Apostles' Creed was not developed at a single church council; instead, it appeared early in church history around AD 200 and gradually developed until AD 750. It wasn't until AD 390 that Rufinus, an early church historian and priest, added the phrase *descendit ad inferna*, which, from Latin, is translated as "He descended into hell."[30] And after Rufinus's addition, it was not included again in any version of the creed until AD 650. It's also not clear what precisely Rufinus meant by this phrase. Did he mean that Jesus went to hell or simply that He went to the grave? Given the uncertainty of Rufinus's meaning and the scattered and late inclusion of the phrase, we should be cautious of leaning too heavily on it as a reflection of the apostles' beliefs.[31]

---

30 Schaff, "The Creeds of Christendom," Vol. 2 chap. 3 section 24.5.2.

31 Schaff, "The Creeds of Christendom," Vol. 1 chap. 2 section 7, footnote 36.

As with any extrabiblical sources of theology, it is important to verify the accuracy of this claim against the pages of Scripture. So, does the Bible support the idea that Christ descended into hell? Scholars commonly appeal to several passages for support: Acts 2:27; Romans 10:6–7; 1 Peter 3:18–20, 4:6; and Ephesians 4:8–9. Let's briefly look at these passages to see if they teach Christ's descent into hell.

> because you will not abandon me in Hades or allow
> your holy one to see decay.
> *Acts 2:27*

The KJV translates the Greek word *hades* as "hell" in Acts 2:27. However, this is unnecessary. The word *hades* can mean "place of the dead,"[32] or it can refer to the grave or death.[33] And to understand it that way makes good sense of this passage, where Paul is quoting from the Old Testament to compare Jesus's death with David's. David is dead and still buried to this day (Acts 2:29), but Christ was not abandoned to the grave. He was raised from it before experiencing fleshly decay (Acts 2:31). The plainest explanation of this text is that it's speaking about Christ being dead, not His descent into hell.

> But the righteousness that comes from faith speaks
> like this: Do not say in your heart, "Who will go up
> to heaven?" that is, to bring Christ down or, "Who
> will go down into the abyss?" that is, to bring Christ
> up from the dead.
> *Romans 10:6–7*

Similarly, in Romans 10:6–7, the phrases "down into the abyss" and "bring Christ up from the dead" are used. The latter phrase is understood as in Acts 2:27 — it speaks of Christ being dead. While some believe that the phrase "down into the abyss" refers to Christ's

---

32 Bauer and Danker, *Greek-English Lexicon*, 19.

33 Barry, "Hades," *The Lexham Bible Dictionary*.

descent into hell, it is again unlikely. "Abyss" is a transliteration of the Greek word *abyssos*.[34] It's not a word that is often used in the New Testament, but it is used extensively in the Septuagint (the Greek translation of the Hebrew Bible) to refer to the depths of the ocean and the realm of the dead.[35] In Romans 10, Paul is trying to demonstrate that there is no need to go to inaccessible places to search for the Word because Christ, the living Word, has come down from heaven and risen from the grave. Therefore, the Word is not inaccessible; rather His message dwells in us through faith. So again, there is no contextual reason to assume Paul means Christ descended into hell.

> For Christ also suffered for sins once for all, the righteous for the unrighteous, that he might bring you to God. He was put to death in the flesh but made alive by the Spirit, in which he also went and made proclamation to the spirits in prison who in the past were disobedient, when God patiently waited in the days of Noah while the ark was being prepared. In it a few — that is, eight people — were saved through water.
> *1 Peter 3:18–20*

> For this reason the gospel was also preached to those who are now dead, so that, although they might be judged in the flesh according to human standards, they might live in the spirit according to God's standards.
> *1 Peter 4:6*

The two passages from 1 Peter are perhaps the most confusing. Both are similar in content. First Peter 3:19 describes how Christ made

---

34   Bauer and Danker, *Greek-English Lexicon*, 2.

35   Grudem, *Systematic Theology*, 730.

"proclamation to the spirits in prison," and 1 Peter 4:6 describes how the gospel has been preached to those who are now dead.

Commentators who are eager to suggest that the Bible teaches Christ's descent into hell believe these texts must teach that Christ descended into hell to make these proclamations. While both texts are difficult to interpret, 1 Peter 3 seems to be teaching that Christ, in spirit, spoke through Noah to the disobedient of his generation while he was building the ark. This explanation makes sense contextually and does not necessitate that Christ descended into hell to preach to spirits in prison.

Similarly, 1 Peter 4 is not speaking about Christ preaching to souls after they have died. In fact, Christ is not even the subject doing the preaching. Rather this verse is teaching that Christians shared the gospel with a group of people who have since died. So again, just as we saw in the previous two verses, these verses from 1 Peter are not teaching Christ's descent into hell.

For it says:

> When he ascended on high,
> he took the captives captive;
> he gave gifts to people.
> But what does "he ascended" mean except that he
> also descended to the lower parts of the earth?
> *Ephesians 4:8–9*

The passage most appealed to by those who support Christ's descent into hell is Ephesians 4:8–9. This is because it uses the language of descent: "But what does 'he ascended' mean except that he also *descended to the lower parts of the earth*" (emphasis added). But does this mean He descended into hell, or could it mean something else?

In Ephesians 4:8, Paul is speaking about Christ's ascension into heaven. Ephesians 4:9 then contrasts His ascension with His coming to earth as a human—He can ascend back to heaven because He first descended to earth. It is not necessary for us to assume that "the lower parts of the earth" means hell or the grave. Paul likely just means the lower parts of creation, which would be the earth. Simply put, this verse is talking about Christ's ascension and incarnation; it does not have His death or a descent into hell in view.

Conclusion

It seems clear that none of these verses support the idea that Christ descended into hell. So what does the Bible say about where Jesus went when He died? Jesus famously said to the thief on the cross, "Truly I tell you, today you will be with me in paradise" (Luke 23:43). There is some debate about what Jesus meant by "paradise," but it surely cannot be taken to mean "hell." Some believe "paradise" refers to Abraham's side, where Lazarus went upon his death (Luke 16:22). This location is clearly not a place of torment as hell is. But interestingly, the word "paradise" is used only two other times in the New Testament, and, in each instance, it refers to heaven (2 Corinthians 12:4, Revelation 2:7).

It seems most natural and likely that upon His death, Jesus's spirit went immediately to heaven, where He joined His Father. However, His body stayed on earth and was buried in the tomb (Luke 23:50–24:3). Then, on the day of His resurrection, His spirit returned to earth to be joined in glory with His body, and He was raised from the dead.

Application

Jesus's experience upon death was not unlike our own. He immediately went to be with His Father in heaven, and His body stayed in the tomb until the two were reunited in His resurrection three days later. When we die, our spirits immediately go to be with the Lord, yet our bodies lie in the ground until the day of Christ's return and our future bodily resurrection. At that moment, our spirits will be reunited with our bodies in glorification, and we will forever dwell with the Lord in our resurrected and glorified bodies.

We can take great comfort knowing that we will not face anything in death that our Savior Himself has not already experienced. In His death, burial, resurrection, and ascension, He has conquered our greatest enemy, death, and has gone before us. For Christ—and now for us—death does not have the final word.

QUESTION 9

If unrepentant sinners have to suffer eternally for sin, why didn't Jesus?

ANSWER:

On the cross, Jesus paid the full penalty that our sins deserved. Because of that, the need for Him to be punished ceased.

RELEVANT PASSAGES:

Matthew 25:46
John 3:16
Colossians 2:14
2 Thessalonians 1:9
Hebrews 9:24–28

Here's the bad news: The Bible tells us that everyone — including you and me — has sinned against God. And because of that, we deserve to spend eternity separated from Him, suffering the punishment for our sins. But there's some good news, too! God loved us so much that He sent His Son, Jesus, to take the punishment for our sins by dying on the cross. Then He rose from death, and if we trust in Him to be our Savior, God promises that we, too, will rise from the grave one day and spend eternity with Him.

Written above is a brief, simple presentation of the gospel, or "good news." Depending on how long you've been a Christian, you've perhaps heard some version of this conversation numerous times or said those words to someone else.

But while everything in that presentation is accurate, it seems to raise a question — one that can linger unnoticed just below the surface of the words themselves. If the punishment we deserve for our sins is eternal suffering and separation from God, and if Jesus came to take that punishment from us, then why isn't Jesus suffering eternally in hell? In fact, not only is Jesus *not* suffering eternally in hell, but He was also exalted to God's right hand (Philippians 2:9)!

Hebrews 12:2 likewise speaks of the "joy" that awaited Jesus after His death on the cross.

In what sense, then, can we meaningfully compare the eternal suffering of sinners with the suffering Jesus endured, which—while severe—was far more limited and was eventually replaced with joy? It's an interesting question! It's also one that the Bible does not directly answer. While the Bible is clear that sin deserves eternal punishment and that Jesus took that punishment in place of sinners, it does not get into the specifics of *how* this all works out. Still, there are biblical passages and principles that can guide our thinking.

To begin, consider what theologian Wayne Grudem observes regarding this question:

> Nothing in the eternal character of God and nothing in the laws God had given for mankind required that there be eternal suffering to pay for man's sins. In fact, if there is eternal suffering, it simply shows that the penalty has never been fully paid, and that the evildoer continues to be a sinner by nature.[36]

Think of it this way: If a person is sentenced to jail for a crime, and then a couple years later you see them walking down the street, what would you conclude? (Let's rule out the scenario that they broke out!) You'd probably conclude that their crime had been paid for. The punishment being given in full, there is no longer any reason for them to remain in jail.

Or consider it in financial terms. Say a person takes out a $20,000 loan. How long will it take them to pay it off? It depends. If they're aggressive, they might be able to pay it off in a couple of years. If they're only making minimum payments on it, it will take far longer. But notice that time is an incidental factor here. The point isn't that they

---

36   Grudem, *Systematic Theology*, 578.

must spend a certain amount of time paying off this loan but rather that they must pay it off, regardless of how long that takes.

Both of these scenarios help illustrate Grudem's point about why unrepentant sinners have to suffer eternally for sin. Remember, God is "the Judge of the whole earth" who does "what is just" (Genesis 18:25). And the "eye for eye, tooth for tooth, hand for hand, foot for foot" law He gave to the nation of Israel (Exodus 21:24) essentially meant that the punishment for offenses must fit the crime. God is just and fair, and therefore, He punishes appropriately, not excessively. What unrepentant sinners deserve, then — like all who have done wrong — is to pay for the wrong they've done. If this punishment is eternal, the implication is that unrepentant sinners can never pay back what they owe God.

But Jesus can.

Think of our prisoner illustration again. If Jesus died to take the punishment for our sins — a punishment we would never be able to pay off — and then we saw Him walking around again, risen from death, what should we conclude? We would rightly conclude that the punishment we deserved has been paid in full, that God's just anger against our sin has been fully exhausted on Jesus. There's nothing left to punish. What we could never accomplish given an eternity, Jesus did on the cross.

A few passages are helpful to consider here. In Romans 8:1, for example, Paul writes that "there is now no condemnation for those in Christ Jesus." It is not that God could condemn us but chooses not to. It's that, for those who "have been justified by faith [and] have peace with God" (Romans 5:1), there is nothing left to condemn.

In Colossians 2:14, Paul uses the imagery of debt, saying that Jesus "erased the certificate of debt, with its obligations, that was against us and opposed to us, and has taken it away by nailing it to the cross." Writing on this passage, commentator Peter O'Brien says that the "debt was impossible to pay, but God dealt with it; he had blotted it out and cancelled the bond by nailing it to the cross. This is a vivid way of saying that because Christ was nailed to the cross, our debt has been completely forgiven."

It is also worth considering Hebrews 9:24–28, a passage in which the author contrasts what high priests in the old covenant would repeatedly do with what Jesus did once and for all. The high priest would enter and leave the Most Holy Place one day a year, year after year, bringing with him the blood of an animal offering. However, Jesus offered *Himself* as a sacrifice and then entered—and remained—in the very presence of God, of which the Most Holy Place was only a shadow.

The crucial point here for the author is the unrepeatable nature of what Jesus did. Human beings, including Jesus, can only die once (Hebrews 9:27). So, if Jesus Himself is a sacrifice for sin, He can only be offered once, not over and over again. He had one death to give and thus one shot to deal with our sin. His sacrifice either removed our sins completely, or it didn't. But praise be to God, it did. Whereas the repeatedly offered sacrifices under the old covenant testified that sin had not been fully dealt with, Jesus's once-for-all sacrifice now testifies that it has.

What Hebrews reminds us is that nothing short of Jesus's death can fully deal with our sin problem. Without Him, our debt is unpayable. No amount of animal sacrifices, offered year after year, could deal with sin. No amount of good works on our end could, either. And that's why punishment is eternal for those who do not repent and turn to Jesus in faith—because only in Him can the demands of God's justice be satisfied on our account.

Application

In the moments after we sin, we can be dominated by fear and guilt. We might labor under the idea that, after what we just did — *again* — we aren't welcome in God's presence. In our minds, we can imagine that He is angry and disappointed and that He needs time to calm down before welcoming us into His presence again. But this is the voice of Satan, "who accuses [us] before our God day and night" (Revelation 12:10). What the gospel tells us is that Jesus has forgiven our "sins and . . . lawless acts" and that "where there is forgiveness of these, there is no longer an offering for sin" (Hebrews 10:17–18). We are as free to approach God on our best days as we are on our worst days. His arms are always open.

Still, this question forces us to acknowledge the seriousness of sin. What we deserve is severe, and we should never forget that. But with this reminder, our hearts should marvel at and be comforted by what Jesus accomplished for us. There is incredible freedom in knowing that we've been forgiven. And there is incredible joy in knowing that eternal life with our loving God awaits us.

QUESTION 10

What is the atonement?

The atonement is the work Christ has done through His life, death, resurrection, and ascension and will do in His return to deal with sin—reconciling sinners to God and renewing creation to its intended state.

RELEVANT PASSAGES:

Leviticus 16
Mark 10:45
Romans 5:6–8
1 Corinthians 5:7, 15:3
2 Corinthians 5:21
Ephesians 5:2
Titus 2:14
Hebrews 9:22
1 Peter 2:24
1 John 3:16

f you were to ask any random person on the street whether things are as they should be, they'd most certainly say no. Everyone recognizes at least some of the evils of the world. Our society is longing for a resolution to its problems and looking in all the wrong places.

What we all need, however, is the hope of the gospel, the heart of which is the atonement.[37]

What is the atonement? This term refers to how Christ—primarily through His sacrificial death—has conquered sin and all its effects, offered sinners reconciliation to God, and promised to renew all creation.

While Christ's atonement is connected to His defeat of sin on the cross, it not only refers to His death but also encompasses the saving benefits He has provided believers through His life, resurrection, ascension, and return. Furthermore, while human beings are the ones who experience the gift of salvation, the hope of the atonement is not just for us but for all of creation, as all creation suffers from the effects of sin (Romans 8:19–22) and will one day be redeemed. Therefore,

---

37   Treat, *The Atonement: An Introduction*, 7.

this chapter will speak of the atonement holistically, exploring how all of Christ's work—from His incarnation to His return—has been ordained to deal with sin and its effects.

It can be extremely helpful when trying to wrap your head around the doctrine of the atonement to distinguish between *what Christ accomplished* and *how He accomplished it.*[38] These two can easily get muddied in our minds. It's common to overemphasize *what Christ accomplished* at the expense of understanding *how* He accomplished it, which really should be at the heart of any discussion of the atonement.

We'll begin by first attempting to answer the question of *how* Christ accomplished atonement before discussing what Christ accomplished in the atonement.

How Did Christ Accomplish Atonement?

So how did Christ conquer sin and all its effects and reconcile us to the Father? He died in our place for our sins (1 Corinthians 15:3, 1 Peter 2:24). Theologians call this substitution. This truth of Christ dying or suffering for us is seen throughout the pages of the New Testament and has its roots in the Old Testament sacrificial system. You can find a list of some of the many verses that teach the truth of substitution in Appendix A.

There are two primary elements to substitution, and by exploring these elements, we can better understand *how* Christ's substitutionary death achieved our salvation.

1. *Christ died in our place.*

First, Christ took our place on the cross, taking the punishment, judgment, wrath, and death we deserved. Ever since the Fall, sin has plagued all of creation. It created a separation between man and a holy God (Genesis 3:23–24, Isaiah 59:2). Romans 3:23

---

38   Treat, *The Atonement: An Introduction*, 38.

reminds us that "all have sinned and fall short of the glory of God." God does not overlook sin. Those who sin receive the wrath of God (John 3:36). They are punished with death (Romans 6:23) and eternal destruction away from the presence of the Lord (2 Thessalonians 1:9).

This was our destiny until Christ died as our substitute. In dying as our substitute (Romans 5:8), He bore our sins (1 Peter 2:24), became a curse for us (Galatians 3:13), and gave Himself as a ransom for us (Mark 10:45). He took upon Himself the wrath of God and received the punishment and death that were supposed to be ours.

2. *Christ gave us what was His.*

Second, He gave us what was His—His righteousness (2 Corinthians 5:21), His Spirit (Romans 8:1–11), and adoption by His Father (Romans 8:15–17). Christ lived a perfect life of obedience, fulfilling the law of God (Matthew 5:17) and never sinning (1 Peter 2:22, Hebrews 4:15, 1 John 3:5). Living a life of righteousness was something only He could do, but it's necessary for fellowship with God (Matthew 5:48, James 2:10). We cannot approach God without righteousness. But in dying as our substitute, Jesus, who did not know sin, was made "to be sin for us, so that in him we might become the righteousness of God" (2 Corinthians 5:21). Now, those who have faith in Christ have been clothed in His righteousness (Romans 3:22, 1 Corinthians 1:30), and when God looks upon us, He doesn't see our sinfulness; instead, He sees us in Christ as righteous and holy.

These two glorious truths of substitution help us understand *how* Christ's substitutionary death achieved our salvation: Christ not only died in our place for our sins, but He also gave us His righteousness.

French Reformer John Calvin captures this marvelous truth by referring to it as "the wonderful exchange":

> This is the wonderful exchange which, out of his measureless benevolence, he has made with us; that . . . by taking on our mortality, he has conferred his immortality upon us, that, receiving our poverty unto himself, he has transferred his wealth to us; that taking the weight of our iniquity upon himself (which oppressed us), he has clothed us with his righteousness.[39]

What Did Christ Accomplish in the Atonement?

With an understanding of *how* Christ accomplished the atonement, let's now turn to *what* He accomplished through His work. In dying in our place for our sins, Christ's death accomplished many purposes that God had ordained. There isn't room in this chapter to explore all of Christ's glorious achievements, but let's look at some of the most prominent.

Christ made propitiation for our sins.

"Propitiation" means "the turning away of wrath by an offering." In relation to Christ, He was the propitiation for our sins through His death, which satisfied the wrath of God, thus removing the wrath from us (1 John 4:10, ESV).

Christ offers us expiation and forgiveness.

"Expiation" means "to cover or cleanse sin." It represents the idea that because of Christ's death on the cross, our sin has been cleansed and removed by the grace of God. Forgiveness is a legal act of God in which He removes the charges against

---

39 Calvin, *Institutes of the Christian Religion*, 1362.

the sinner. God has provided forgiveness of our sins through Jesus Christ (Acts 13:38, Ephesians 1:7). Through expiation and forgiveness, we are both positionally and experientially freed from the penalty of sin.

Christ claims victory.

When God created Adam and Eve, He gave them a mandate to exercise rule or dominion over all the earth (Genesis 1:26–28). Since they were made in the image of God, they reflected God to the rest of the created order. This perfect reign of man with God was short lived, as sin was quickly introduced, submersing the world into the kingdom of darkness (Colossians 1:13). But through His life and death, Christ claimed victory over sin and Satan. He destroyed the works of the devil (1 John 3:8, Hebrews 2:14), and "He disarmed the rulers and authorities and disgraced them publicly; he triumphed over them in him" (Colossians 2:15).

Christ reconciles us to God.

Mankind is separated from God because of our sinfulness, and in order for us to have fellowship with God, Jesus had to die and provide reconciliation (2 Corinthians 5:18–19, Romans 5:10). Reconciliation is the restoration of this relationship. When Christ died on the cross, He accomplished what theologians call "potential reconciliation" — this refers to Christ giving the world the *potential* to be reconciled to God. Actual reconciliation, on the other hand, is realized when believers place their faith in Jesus for salvation.

Christ redeems us.

All of humanity is in bondage to sin and Satan (John 8:34, 1 John 5:19), and as a result, we need someone to redeem us from that bondage. This concept closely relates with the idea of a ransom. Jesus Christ came to give His life as our ransom and to redeem us from the bondage of sin (Mark 10:45, Hebrews 2:15, Ephesians 1:7). Redemption has provided believers with eternal life (Revelation 5:9–10), righteousness (Romans 5:17), freedom from the curse of the Law (Galatians 3:13), adoption into God's family (Galatians 4:5), and deliverance from the bondage of sin (Titus 2:14, 1 Peter 1:14–18).

Christ justifies us.

Justification is a legal act of God through which He considers our sins forgiven, considers Christ's righteousness as belonging to us, and declares us righteous in His sight (Romans 3:23–24, 5:1; Philippians 3:9). The righteousness of Christ is applied to us, and we are considered justified immediately after we place our faith in Jesus Christ (Galatians 2:16, Romans 3:21–22, 25–26).

Christ sanctifies us.

Theologian Anthony Hoekema defines sanctification as:

> "that gracious operation of the Holy Spirit, involving our responsible participation, by which He delivers us as justified sinners from the pollution of sin, renews our entire nature according to the image of God, and enables us to live lives that are pleasing to Him."[40]

While there is a progressive element to sanctification, we can be sure that the Spirit will bring this work to completion (Philippians 1:6), because by His blood, Christ has sanctified His people (Hebrews 9:13–14, 10:14, 13:12).

---

40   Dieter et al., Five Views on Sanctification, 61.

Christ will one day glorify us.

Glorification is the final aspect of salvation, involving the perfection of believers, in which their bodies are finally freed from the presence of sin. It involves the transformation of the whole person — body and soul — into the likeness of Christ and His glory (Philippians 3:20–21). At the return of Christ, the bodies of believers who have died will be resurrected and reunited with their souls (1 Thessalonians 4:16–17), and those who are alive will be changed in an instant into His likeness (Romans 8:11; see also 2 Corinthians 5:1–10, Philippians 3:20–21).

Application

The wonders of the atonement are too vast for us to mine as finite creatures, and its applications are many. Pastor Jeremy Treat, in his wonderfully brief yet profoundly rich study of the atonement says, "Through his death on the cross, Jesus takes our broken lives and makes them whole again . . . [and] while Christ makes us whole again, the greatest accomplishment of the cross is that we are made at-one with God. And that is the key."[41]

Whatever brokenness you experience in life has been, can be, or will be healed by the atonement of Jesus Christ. There is no pain or problem that God did not intend to heal through the life, death, resurrection, ascension, and return of Christ. So, in your weakness, turn to Him for life, healing, and reconciliation with the Father.

---

41 Treat, *The Atonement: An Introduction*, 158.

QUESTION 11

For whom did Jesus die?

ANSWER:

While Jesus paid the penalty for sin with His substitutionary death on the cross, all true Christians believe that this payment is limited, or only applied, to those who by grace have placed their faith in Him. There is debate around the reason why this payment is limited, and the most common positions include limited atonement, unlimited atonement, and a multi-intentioned view of the atonement.

RELEVANT PASSAGES:

John 1:29
1 John 2:2

 reviously in this book, we've answered questions related to the nature of Christ's death, and we've seen clearly that through His death, Christ paid for sins (Colossians 2:13–14). But a simple question related to that payment has caused division and confusion among Christians for hundreds, if not thousands, of years: Did Christ die for all people?

When attempting to answer this question, theologians speak of the extent and the effect of the atonement. In a very simple sense, the discussion of *extent* revolves around whether Christ died for all people or just for the elect, those whom He chose to be saved. Meanwhile, the question of *effect* has to do with Christ's death actually securing salvation for particular individuals.

TABLE 1:
The Atonement: Extent and Effect

The **extent** of the atonement	Answers the question: *Who did Christ die for—all people or just the elect?*
The **effect** of the atonement	Answers the question: *What did Christ's death do? Did it secure salvation for all people or just the elect?*

There are four common positions on this issue: universalism, unlimited atonement, limited atonement, and the multi-intentioned view of the atonement. Throughout this chapter, we will compare these four positions by examining what they claim about the extent and the effect of the atonement.

Position 1: Universalism

The first position is universalism. Universalism is the belief that the atonement is unlimited in both extent and effect. In other words, universalists believe that Jesus died for all people, and all people experience and enjoy the effects of that death whether they believe in Him or not. Theologically, this means that the saving benefits Jesus accomplished in His life and death are applied to all people who have ever lived, regardless of their personal expression of belief in Christ.

However, this position is incompatible with a high view of Scripture that believes the Word to be inspired by God, inerrant, and authoritative for all of life, for Scripture clearly teaches that the saving benefits secured by Christ in His life and death are only applied by grace to those who express faith in Christ (John 3:16, Ephesians 2:8–9, Romans 10:9–10). Additionally, Scripture makes it abundantly clear that not all will be saved and experience eternal life with God (Matthew 7:13–14, 22–23; 25:46; 2 Thessalonians 1:9; Revelation 20:15).

Since the remaining three positions all believe that not everyone will be saved, they all understand the atonement of Christ to be limited in some way. What sets these positions apart from universalism is that they all agree that the atonement is limited by one's belief in Christ. John 3:16 says, "For God loved the world in this way: He gave his one and only Son, so that *everyone who believes in him* will not perish but have eternal life" (emphasis added). All of the remaining positions we will survey believe that the atonement is limited in effect to those who believe.

Position 2: Unlimited Atonement

The second view of the atonement we'll examine is referred to as unlimited atonement. Advocates of unlimited atonement believe that God loves all people and desires for all people to be saved, so He sent Christ to pay for the sins of all people.[42] This belief results in an atonement that is unlimited *in extent* but limited *in effect*. In other words, those who hold this view believe that Jesus paid for the sins of all people, making salvation possible for all people. But an individual does not experience the saving effects of Christ's life and death until they put their faith in Christ. The intention of the atonement, then, is to make salvation possible for all people.

Advocates of this position believe that the limitation of belief is imposed by mankind. In other words, men have the free will to accept or decline the offer of salvation that God makes to them through the proclamation of the gospel.

Position 3: Limited Atonement

The third view of the atonement, limited atonement, is often spoken of in contrast to unlimited atonement. Limited atonement is the belief that both the extent and the effect of the atonement are restricted to the elect. Again, similar to unlimited atonement, belief is the limiting factor of the atonement. But proponents of limited atonement believe that the extent of that belief is limited by God instead of man. God chooses some people for salvation (Ephesians 1:3–5) and by grace gives them the gift of faith (Ephesians 2:8–10). They then express faith in Christ and confess Him as Lord (Romans 10:9–10), and as a result, experience the saving effects of Christ's work.

Proponents of limited atonement are careful to point out *that the atonement has a singular intention*: to secure and accomplish the salvation of the elect.[43] Since this purpose is singular and limited to the

---

42 Ware, "Extent of the Atonement," 2.

43 Berkhof, *Systematic Theology*, 494.

elect, God's provision in Christ (i.e., the extent) must also be singular and limited. Therefore, Christ died on behalf of only those who were unconditionally chosen to believe in Him.

Position 4: Multi-Intentioned Atonement

The final view of the atonement is the multi-intentioned view of the atonement. It is sometimes understood to be a mediating position between unlimited and limited atonement and, as such, has also been referred to as "unlimited-limited atonement." This position understands God to have multiple intentions in the death of Christ,[44] as opposed to the singular intentions of the limited and unlimited views. Theologian Bruce Ware suggests that God has five intentions in the death of Christ:

1. To secure the salvation of the elect
2. To pay "the penalty for the sin of all people making it possible *for all who believe to be saved*" (emphasis added)[45]
3. To secure the offer of salvation to everyone
4. To provide a basis for the condemnation of those who reject the gospel upon hearing it
5. To reconcile all things to the Father[46]

Some of these intentions, such as securing the salvation of the elect, mirror limited atonement, while others, such as paying the penalty for the sin of all people, align more closely with unlimited atonement. This is why the multi-intentioned view can be thought of as a mediating position.

Similar to unlimited atonement, this position sees the atonement as unlimited in extent. However, the key distinction here is that instead of seeing Jesus's death as making it possible for all people to be saved, advocates maintain that while Christ paid the penalty of sin for all people, His death only made it possible for *those who believe* to be

---

44 Ware, "Extent of the Atonement," 3.

45 Ware, "Extent of the Atonement," 3.

46 Ware, "Extent of the Atonement," 3.

TABLE 2:
Four Views of Atonement

	EXTENT	EFFECT	KEY TAKEAWAY	VERSES USED TO SUPPORT THE POSITION	OTHER CONSIDERATIONS	HISTORICAL ADHERENTS	GENERAL DENOMINATIONAL ADHERENTS
UNIVERSALISM	Unlimited	Unlimited	Christ died for all people. No matter what one believes about Him, they will be saved.	John 12:32 Romans 5:12–21; 11:32 1 Timothy 2:4; 4:10	This position is not compatible with a high view of Scripture; therefore, it is not compatible with true Christianity.	Origen John Murray George de Benneville	Unitarian Universalists
UNLIMITED ATONEMENT	Unlimited	Limited (by man)	Christ made salvation possible for all people, but one must put their faith in Him to experience salvation.	John 3:16 2 Corinthians 5:14–19 Romans 5:6–8 1 Timothy 2:4–6; 4:10 2 Peter 2:1; 3:9 1 John 2:2; 4:14	N/A	Jacobus Arminius David Allen	Methodists Wesleyans Nazarenes Churches of God Assemblies of God Some Baptists
LIMITED ATONEMENT	Limited	Limited (by God)	God has ordained His chosen people for salvation. Christ died for these chosen individuals, who then experience salvation when they place their faith in Christ.	John 6:37–44; 10:11, 15 Acts 20:28 Romans 8:31–39 2 Corinthians 5:15 Ephesians 5:25 Titus 2:14	N/A	John Calvin Louis Berkhof John Knox John Piper	Reformed churches Presbyterians Reformed Baptists
MULTI-INTENTIONED ATONEMENT	Unlimited	Limited (by God)	Christ paid the penalty of sin for all people, but His death only made it possible for those who believe to be saved.	John 3:18; 6:35–40; 10:11, 15 Acts 20:28 Romans 8:31–39 2 Corinthians 5:15 Ephesians 5:25 Colossians 1:19–20 1 Timothy 4:10 Titus 2:14 2 Peter 2:1 1 John 2:2	This position is sometimes understood to be a mediating position between unlimited and limited atonement.	Moses Amyraut Bruce Ware	Some Baptists Some Bible churches

saved.[47] Yet the way in which the atonement is limited is similar to the position of limited atonement. The limitation of belief is imposed upon people by God rather than man, and so God only applies the saving benefits of Christ's work to those whom He chose before the foundation of the world to be saved.

Application

Regardless of the reason *why* we believe the application of Christ's substitutionary death to be limited, all true believers understand its application to be limited to those who believe. And for those of us who believe, we can praise God for Christ Jesus in whom we have redemption and the forgiveness of our sins. "Christus Victor (Amen)," a wonderful modern hymn, captures the truths of the atonement and gives us a response for our hearts to sing:

---

47   Ware, "Extent of the Atonement," 3.

O Most High, King of the ages
Great I AM, God of wonders
By the blood You have redeemed us
Led us through mighty waters
Our strength, our song, our sure salvation
Now to the Lamb upon the throne
Be blessing, honor, glory, power
For the battle You have won
Hallelujah! Amen

O Most High, dwelling among us
Son of Man sent for sinners
By Your blood You have redeemed us
Spotless Lamb, mighty Savior
Who lived, who died, who rose victorious

Now to the Lamb upon the throne
Be blessing, honor, glory, power
For the battle You have won
Hallelujah![48]

48   Papa et al., "Christus Victor (Amen)."

QUESTION 12

What does it mean to know Christ crucified?

ANSWER:

To "know Christ crucified" is to remember the utter humility Jesus Christ displayed by dying on a cross and to live out the same self-sacrificial love in our daily lives.

RELEVANT PASSAGES:

1 Corinthians 1:18–2:16
Luke 9:23
Philippians 2:1–18

I n 1 Corinthians 2:2, the Apostle Paul writes, "I decided to know nothing among you except Jesus Christ and him crucified." Why does Paul feel the need to emphasize that he knows nothing apart from Jesus Christ crucified as he writes to the Corinthian church? Why is it significant that the recipients of Paul's letter should not only think about Jesus but should also think about His crucifixion? As we will see in this chapter, when Paul writes about knowing Christ crucified, he is calling us to remember the utter humility and service our Savior displayed by dying on a cross.

Shame into Glory

In the Greco-Roman world, there was perhaps no greater shame than to be put to death on a cross. The Romans carefully crafted the execution style of crucifixion to be entirely degrading; it was the most shameful, undignified way to die. In addition to the shame of publicly hanging on a cross, Jesus Christ endured the humiliation of the Roman soldiers, who shoved a crown of thorns upon His head, spat in His face, mocked Him in front of the crowds, and whipped Him publicly. And He withstood it all, knowing all the while that He was the only innocent man to ever live on earth. If there was one person who did not deserve that kind of punishment, it was Jesus.

Why did He withstand it? Why didn't He just stop it all? He certainly had the authority and power to end this humiliation (Matthew 26:52–54, John 19:11). But Jesus submitted Himself to death because He knew that only through the most horrific means of death could the most beautiful redemption come about. By becoming the suffering Servant (Isaiah 53:4–6), He also became the Conqueror over death, the King of kings, and the Lord over all. This is God's upside-down kingdom—a phrase theologians use to describe the theme of humility and redemption throughout the Bible. God's kingdom is one in which "the last will be first, and the first last" (Matthew 20:16).

Our world has always glorified strength and power, but God gives Christians a new standard of living. When He commands us to take up our cross daily and follow Him (Luke 9:23), He is asking us to step into His total humility and sacrifice. We give up the worldly standards of dignity and status that used to control our lives and our identity. Instead, we take on the humility of Christ—the One who served others and obeyed God, even to the point of dying on a cross (Philippians 2:8). When we step into Christ's example of self-sacrificial humility, we do not find the shame of this world; we find the freedom of God and citizenship in His upside-down kingdom.

God's Wisdom

Let's look at the context of the rest of Paul's letter. First Corinthians was written to the church in Corinth, which was having major issues within their church body—from unchecked immorality to deep division among its members. The Corinthians knew the message of the gospel, yet they refused to relinquish their old, worldly ways.

Among the ancient Greeks, wisdom was considered incredibly virtuous and honorable. But the Greeks' standards of "wisdom" were not the same as God's. There was a dignity in belonging to the philosophical sects of different Greek scholars, but it created much division among the people. In other words, it was like an entire culture being divided by knowing an inside joke — those who "get it" and those who "didn't get it." And this mindset was creeping into the church. They were divided by which leader they preferred, saying, "I belong to Paul" or "I belong to Apollos" (1 Corinthians 1:12).

Because of this, Paul wrote a letter to the church, rebuking them for forgetting the model of Jesus Christ. Paul asks them, "Hasn't God made the world's wisdom foolish?" (1 Corinthians 1:20). God didn't come to save those who were prideful and authoritative in their worldly knowledge; He came to save those who were humble enough to place their hope in the cross of Jesus Christ.

Of course, this seems like foolishness to the world, but those who belong to God's upside-down kingdom recognize that it is actually the most incredible wisdom, power, and dignity that a person could possess. By dying to yourself — your worldly standards of power, knowledge, and control — you *gain* your life in Jesus Christ, which is the only true life worth living (Matthew 16:25).

Therefore, Paul proclaims that he boasted of no worldly wisdom or humanly power when he proclaimed the message of the gospel to the Corinthians. He says he only preached "Christ crucified" (1 Corinthians 1:23; see also 2:2). The cross — the symbol of complete shame — has now become the very thing that has saved our souls, and realizing this is a kind of wisdom that nothing in this world could ever compare to.

Application

As Christians, we have a new standard of living. Though we once followed the ways of the world, we now follow the example of Christ. Jesus did not take the form of an earthly king who shows brute strength through military power. He took on the form of a Servant who died on the cross for the sake of our sins. And we are called to follow His example, crucifying our former ways as we look to Him.

What we once believed was foolish—humble service to others and obedience to God—is now the model of our lives. He who now lives in us transforms our lives to take on the same approach and seek to live with the same attitude (Galatians 2:20, Philippians 2:5). Therefore, when we remember how Christ took on the shame of the world through the most horrific form of death on a cross, we remember how we are also meant to live our lives: in humble service to Him and, by His grace, free from shame.

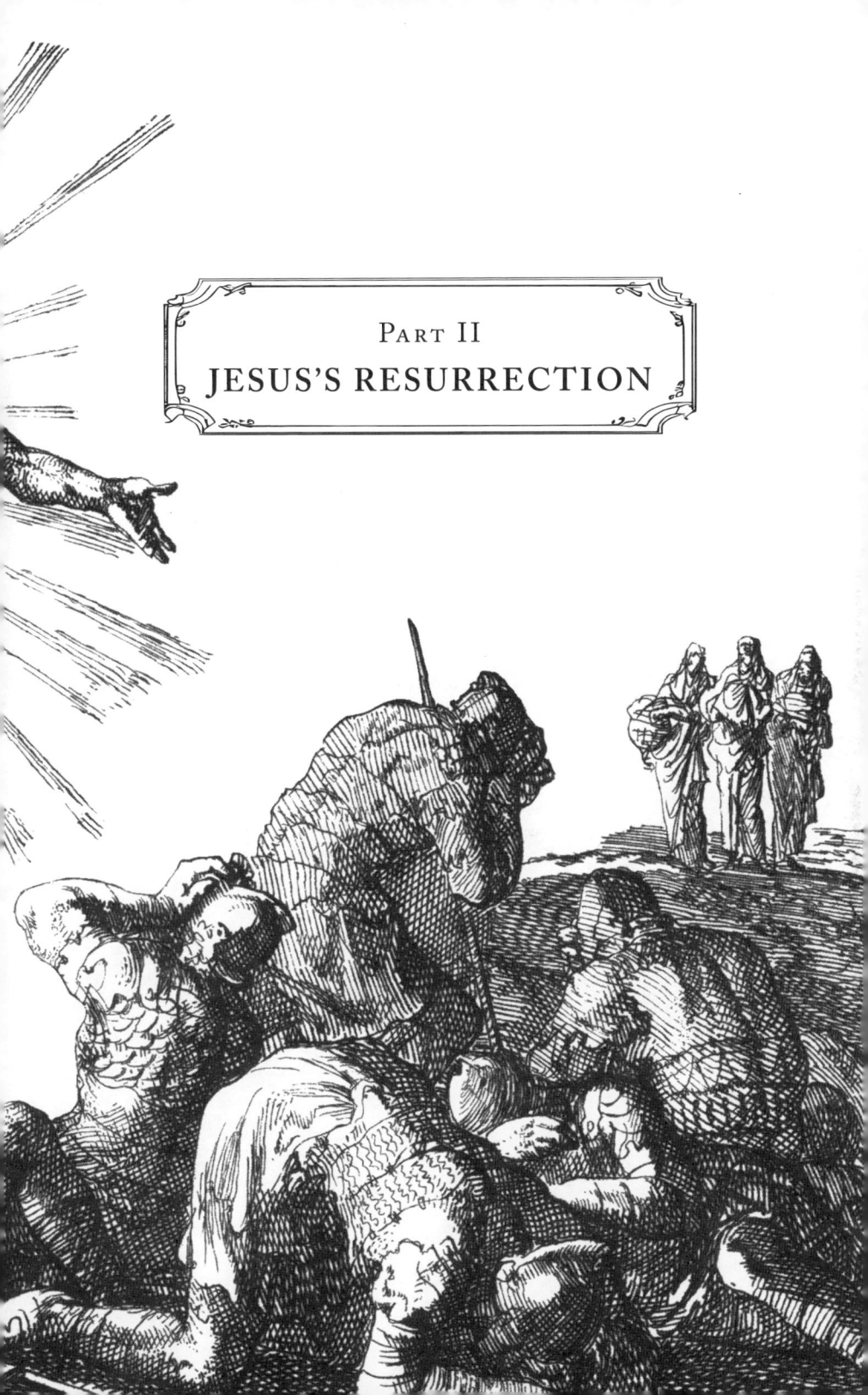

PART II

JESUS'S RESURRECTION

Jesus was crucified.
But now, Jesus has risen!

PART II

JESUS'S RESURRECTION

In Part I of this book, we took a deep dive into questions regarding Jesus's horrific death on the cross. We grappled with the immense suffering Jesus experienced on our behalf and how He willingly succumbed to death so that we would experience eternal life.

After Jesus breathed His last, His body lay in a tomb. A heavy stone was rolled in front of its entrance. Guards were stationed outside the tomb to ensure it would not be disturbed. The disciples had scattered. Jesus's friends and family grieved. The news of Jesus's death had spread throughout Jerusalem. What would happen next?

A miracle.

As women approached the tomb on the day after the Sabbath, something incredible took place. The ground shook, an angel approached, and the stone was rolled away. Then, the angel proclaimed to the women, "Don't be afraid, because I know you are looking for Jesus who was crucified. He is not here. For he has risen, just as he said. Come and see the place where he lay" (Matthew 28:5–6).

Jesus was crucified. But now, Jesus has risen!

The women ran quickly from the tomb with "fear and great joy" (Matthew 28:8). As soon as they set off, they encountered the resurrected Jesus. Their response to the risen Christ was to worship Him and then run to tell others of His resurrection.

Maybe the narrative of the resurrection is familiar to you. You might have heard teachings or sung songs about the stone rolling away and a resurrected Christ exiting the grave. But even if you are familiar with the resurrection accounts in the Gospels, you may still have questions. After all, this narrative does leave us wondering at times.

Why do the Gospels' accounts of the resurrection seem to differ slightly? What was Jesus's resurrection body like? What will our resurrected bodies be like? And what proof is there of Jesus's resurrection? This section will answer all of these questions and more.

In Part II, you will learn about what the resurrection is and how Jesus's resurrection is described in Scripture. You will behold the divine power of Jesus that was on glorious display on resurrection morning, and you will learn about the power of the resurrection for you. This section will leave you in awe of Jesus and longing for the day you will join Him in the resurrection in eternity.

QUESTION 13

In light of Christ's resurrection, what happens to us after we die?

_____

ANSWER:

After death, our souls will be with Jesus in heaven. But upon Christ's glorious Second Coming, He will resurrect our bodies to be reunited with our souls. Thus we will enter into eternal glory in resurrected bodies.

RELEVANT PASSAGES:

Daniel 12:2
Luke 24
1 Corinthians 15
1 Thessalonians 4:13–18
Revelation 20–21

n 2023, the biggest box office movie of the year was Greta Gerwig's satirical comedy *Barbie*.[49] During one of the scenes, the Barbies are having a dance party in Barbie's Dreamhouse. While all the characters are enjoying themselves without a care in the world, Barbie suddenly blurts out this outlandish comment: "Do you guys ever think about dying?"[50] All the music, all the dancing, all the laughter stop abruptly. Everyone looks at Barbie with confused and concerned faces, because as Barbies, they've never had to think about mortal realities.

Death is not something we usually enjoy thinking about, nor does it make for lighthearted conversations. But thinking about what happens to our bodies and our souls when we die not only gives us a proper perspective on life—it also helps us understand our Savior's death and resurrection.

In this chapter, we will explore what happens to us after we die. Then, we will examine two false beliefs about the afterlife that Christians have sometimes held. By looking at these misconceptions, we will gain a better understanding of what our resurrection will

---

49   IMDbPro, "2023 Worldwide Box Office."
50   *Barbie*, directed by Greta Gerwig (Warner Bros., 2023).

truly be like. And through it all, we will be reminded that we no longer have to fear what will happen to us when we die because of the certainty of Christ's victory over death and His promise to bring us into everlasting life.

God's Design for Our Bodies and Plan for Our Resurrection

Let's begin this conversation by looking at God's design for our bodies. The Bible teaches that the body and the soul are both essential components to a person's identity. That is why death—the separation of the soul from the body—is so tragic. It is not God's original design; it is a terrible consequence of the Fall.

For believers, death means that our physical bodies will stay on earth while our souls will go to heaven. But that is not our permanent destination. When Jesus resurrects all people at His Second Coming, He will reestablish God's original design for us: Our physical bodies will be raised from the dead to reunite with our souls and enter into the new creation (Revelation 21). This is the historic Christian view.

However, some people have come to different conclusions about what happens to us after we die. These conclusions are not supported by Scripture, but they have remained popular, even among Christians. Let's take a look at two of these false beliefs about the afterlife in order to understand the significance of what the Bible truly teaches.

False Beliefs About the Afterlife

Purgatory

One prominent belief about what happens to Christians when they die concerns purgatory. This view asserts that after death, a Christian will go to an intermediate state called purgatory, where their soul will be purified from its evil and sinfulness before it reaches heaven. According to this belief, purgatory is a place that exists in between life and death where people may endure years, decades, or even centuries of purification before entering heaven. Proponents of purgatory claim that once one's soul has been purified, then they will be able to enjoy heaven forever.

The concept of purgatory, however, cannot coexist with the truth of the gospel, for it assumes that Christ's salvation is not sufficient to cleanse someone of their sins and that sinners need additional salvation outside of Jesus. But this is *not* what the Bible teaches. Instead, the New Testament adamantly declares that Christians have been cleansed from our past sins (2 Peter 1:9) and that Jesus has cleansed our consciences (Hebrews 9:14). In other words, He has paid it all on our behalf, and though we may continue to struggle with sin in this life, no amount of sin can change a believer's status before God as being righteous in Christ. For those who trust in Jesus, there is no need for purgatory, for there is nothing left to atone for. Our sins have been covered in Him.

Soul Sleep

Another false belief about what happens to Christians after they die is the idea of soul sleep. This is the belief that when a person dies, both their body and soul will "sleep," or live in unconscious oblivion, until Christ returns and resurrects all people from the dead. According to proponents of soul sleep, the resurrection that will take place when Christ returns will simply involve Jesus "waking up" all people from the unconscious state they succumbed to with their death.

This belief derives from a misunderstanding of passages in the New Testament that use the term "asleep" to refer to believers who have died (1 Thessalonians 4:13, 1 Corinthians 15:20, John 11:11). But these passages use the analogy of falling asleep not to say that our souls will be unconscious but to communicate the hopeful truth that death, like sleep, is not permanent but something we will wake up from.

According to the Bible, when we die, our souls go to heaven (Philippians 1:23), where we will remain with Him until His Second Coming. During this time, we will not be asleep. Instead, our souls will be consciously worshiping and enjoying fellowship with Christ as we wait for the day when He will return to earth to restore all things and usher in the new heaven and new earth.

Equipped with the knowledge that both purgatory and soul sleep propose false ideas about what will happen to us when we die, we can come to the joyful realization that we don't have to fear death. This is because we know that when we die, our souls will be with the One who loves us eternally and reigns over all things. Indeed, He is our hope in life and death.

Application

This understanding of our eternal future gives us a greater assurance in our faith, helps us recognize the importance of God's creation of both our souls and our bodies, and teaches us how to live set apart from the rest of the world. Even as we live in our broken, sick, and dying bodies in this current life, we live with the hope that we will one day be with Jesus forevermore — first as souls that will dwell with Him in heaven and then as reunited bodies and souls that will dwell with Him in His glorious new creation (Revelation 21–22).

Therefore, we can think, act, and speak in a way that communicates the hope of Jesus's resurrection with the rest of the world. We can profess the gospel with urgency, inviting others to trust in Him so that they, too, can enjoy this glorious future in Christ. And finally, we can remember that we need not grieve without hope as we mourn the loss of our brothers and sisters in Christ who have died before us, for we can have sure confidence that they are with their Savior even now, and we will worship Him alongside them one day soon.

QUESTION 14

In light of Christ's resurrection, what will our resurrected bodies be like?

_____

ANSWER:

Christ's resurrected body foreshadows what our resurrected bodies will be like when He brings us into the new creation. With reunited and perfected bodies and souls, we will enter into the new creation Jesus ushers in.

RELEVANT PASSAGES:

Luke 24:36–43
John 20:26–27
1 Corinthians 15:35–54
Philippians 3:21
Revelation 20–21

ur bodies feel the consequences of the Fall every day. We live in sick, broken, decaying bodies. Some of us live with bodily disabilities, chronic pain, or terminal sickness. Some of us feel deep-rooted insecurity and have never truly felt like we belonged in our bodies. We long for an existence with no more pain, no more suffering, no more sickness. We long for a day when our earthly bodies will be made new.

We exist — both now and in the new creation — as embodied souls. (To learn more about this, check out the answer to Question 13). Our physical bodies are not at war with our souls. They work together to make up our complete being. Therefore, when Jesus resurrects our bodies in the new creation, our souls and our bodies will be reunited together, as they are united right now. However, when our souls and bodies reunite in the resurrection, they will be perfected. What does this mean? Let's take a look at how our bodies will be transformed when Jesus resurrects us and ushers in the new creation. To do this, we will look at Christ's own resurrected body and what it can teach us about our future resurrected state.

What Will Our Resurrected Bodies Be Like?

In order to gain a sense of what our bodies will become in the future resurrection, we need to take a look at what Jesus's body was like when He rose from the dead. In the forty days between His resurrection and His ascension, Jesus spent time traveling around Jerusalem and Galilee, appearing to His disciples and proclaiming His role as the prophesied Messiah and the fulfillment of all Scripture. The way Jesus spent these forty days gives us some insight into the nature of the resurrected bodies we will possess one day. Jesus's body is the firstfruits of the resurrection, allowing us to see what our bodies will truly become when they are resurrected into a perfect state (1 Corinthians 15:20–23). Let's begin by seeing the ways Jesus's resurrected body is similar to our current earthly bodies.

Our Resurrected Bodies Will Be Similar to Our Earthly Bodies

First, Christ's resurrected body was indeed physical. He was not just a spirit or a ghost. Luke 24:36–43 explains how Jesus's disciples were startled when He appeared to them because they thought they were seeing a ghost. But Jesus corrected them — ghosts do not have flesh and bones! Jesus had a physical body that could be touched, could speak, and could digest food much like our current, earthly bodies.

Second, Jesus's resurrected body was similar to His earthly body in that He possessed the same identifiable qualities. When Jesus appeared to His disciples, they could look at Him and recognize their friend with whom they had traveled for three years. Even by the sound of His voice, Mary Magdalene was able to recognize that the person standing before her was Jesus Christ (John 20:16). The scars on His hands, sides, and feet remained as identifiable qualities as well. While there are multiple occurrences when Jesus appeared to His disciples and they did not recognize Him, we can conclude that these moments were due to the miraculous working of the Holy Spirit to conceal

Jesus's identity until the proper time of His revelation rather than a physical change to Jesus's appearance.

These are two ways that Jesus's resurrected body hints at what our own resurrected bodies will be like, but let's now redirect our attention to two ways our resurrected bodies will be *different* from earthly bodies. To do so, we will again look at the example of Jesus.

Our Resurrected Bodies Will Be Different from Our Earthly Bodies

The greatest difference between our earthly bodies and our resurrected bodies, however, will be this: Resurrected bodies are not bound to the physical limitations of death. As we all know, our current bodies feel the weight of sin's greatest consequence—death. Our bodies ache, decay, and become sick. But the Wycliffe Bible Encyclopedia explains that when our bodies are resurrected, they will adapt to the conditions of heaven.[51] Our resurrected bodies will be transformed into eternal, perfect, and pure bodies because they will enter into a realm that is eternal, perfect, and pure. There will be no more death, no more grief, no more crying, and no more pain (Revelation 21:4).

Our Future Resurrection Should Impact Our Lives Today

So, how does understanding what our bodies will become in the resurrection inform how we treat and care for our bodies right now? Our current earthly bodies—though they feel the physical effects of the Fall—are nevertheless made in the image of God. They are created for a purpose. They contribute to our unique identities. They are used to serve, worship, and glorify God. Human bodies are essential to God's good design, and they will not be neglected once we die. They will simply be perfected, transformed, and made new. Therefore, we can look forward to our resurrected bodies even while continuing to care for and honor the earthly bodies we currently possess.

---

51   Pfeiffer et al., eds., "Spiritual Body, Terrestrial Body."

In 1 Corinthians 15:35–54, the Apostle Paul writes the Bible's most exhaustive commentary on our future resurrection, and he summarizes the resurrection like this: We are *born of Adam*, but we will be *raised with Jesus Christ*. We are born into corruption, but we will be raised in incorruption (1 Corinthians 15:42). We are born into dishonor, but we will be raised in glory (1 Corinthians 15:43). We are born into weakness, but we will be raised in power (1 Corinthians 15:43). We are born into natural, earthly bodies, but we will be raised in heavenly, spiritual bodies (1 Corinthians 15:44).

The resurrection will not give us completely different bodies. The resurrection will take our current bodies, which can only belong to earth, and transform them into bodies that can enter the new creation and the presence of our Almighty God. And when that occurs, we will praise God for His incredible power and grace, repeating the words of the Apostle Paul: "Death has been swallowed up in victory. Where, death, is your victory? Where, death, is your sting?" (1 Corinthians 15:54–55).

Application

At the end of Paul's commentary on the resurrection in 1 Corinthians 15, he encourages the Corinthian believers with this last word: "Therefore, my dear brothers and sisters, be steadfast, immovable, always excelling in the Lord's work, because you know that your labor in the Lord is not in vain" (1 Corinthians 15:58). When we see all that our bodies are promised to become in the resurrection, there might be times when we despair at the current state of our imperfect bodies. But Paul's commission to the Corinthian believers remains the same for us. The way you serve the Lord through your current, physical body is not in vain. We remain steadfast to the work Jesus Christ has called us to *because* we have such an incredible hope for our future.

The gift of resurrected bodies we will receive in the new creation is something we could have never deserved. Yet because of Christ's sacrifice and victory over death, He willingly gives us this promise. Therefore, we seek to glorify Him with every moment of our lives as we look forward to the day when our bodies will be transformed to live in His presence forever.

QUESTION 15

Do the resurrection accounts contradict each other?

ANSWER:

Though the Gospels have small differences between their resurrection accounts, these differences neither contradict nor undermine the truth of the main story the authors were telling.

RELEVANT PASSAGES:

Matthew 28:1–9
Mark 16:1–8
Luke 24:1–12
John 20:1–18

f you and your friends all decided to share about the same experience with someone, you would probably go about telling that story in different ways. The details might vary, but the main point of the story would remain the same.

Such is the case with the four Gospel accounts in Scripture. Matthew, Mark, Luke, and John all write about the resurrection. And while they all tell the same story, there are some differences between the way they each tell that story. However, these differences don't cause the four Gospel accounts to contradict each other. A case can be made for the differences in these accounts, demonstrating that the Gospels can be trusted even with their varying details.

Before we discuss some of the differences between the Gospel accounts, it's helpful to know that these differences are intentional. Each Gospel writer wrote for a particular audience and had specific truths or themes they sought to convey to that audience. Therefore, the differences within their accounts can encourage us in our study of the Gospels as we seek to discover why the Gospel writers selected particular details and words.

While the Gospel writers highlighted different details, we also must remember that they all aimed to tell one consistent story. They were concerned with telling the story of Jesus, affirming His deity, and proclaiming the good news of His death and resurrection. In reading their accounts of Christ's resurrection, we see the writers accomplishing that major emphasis. Each Gospel writer reveals the truth of the empty grave, proclaiming that Jesus has conquered death and is, in fact, alive. This teaches us that though there are differences between the Gospels, these are secondary in light of the main story the authors were telling.

With this in mind, let's consider some ways the Gospel accounts differ when speaking about the resurrection. In this chapter, we will look at three main differences found within Matthew, Mark, Luke, and John: the time of day that the women went to the tomb, the names and number of these women, and the number of the angels present at the empty tomb.

1. The Time of Day

One difference is the description of the time of day in which the women go to visit the tomb. Matthew writes that it was as the day "was dawning" (Matthew 28:1). Mark says it was "at sunrise" (Mark 16:2). Luke writes that it was "very early in the morning" (Luke 24:1). And John says that it was "still dark" (John 20:1). While these could be described as discrepancies, what is actually happening is that the writers were using different words to speak to the same time of day. It is also possible that John, in particular, was describing when Mary Magdalene left to go to the tomb instead of the other Gospel writers, who wrote about when the women arrived.

2. The Names and Number of the Women

Another difference has to do with the names of the women at the empty tomb and how many were there. Matthew writes that "Mary Magdalene and the other Mary" went to the tomb (Matthew 28:1). Mark also writes that Mary Magdalene and Mary "the mother of

James" went to the tomb, yet he also adds a woman named Salome to the group (Mark 16:1–2). Luke writes that after seeing the empty tomb, "Mary Magdalene, Joanna, Mary the mother of James, and the other women with them were telling the apostles these things" (Luke 24:10). John, however, writes that Mary Magdalene saw the empty tomb and went on to see the risen Christ (John 20:1).

While there are differences between these accounts, it is probable that all the women named in all four Gospels went to the tomb. Matthew may have cited two and John one, but this doesn't mean that *only* those women were present. In fact, in John's Gospel, when Mary tells Peter about the empty grave, she says, "They've taken the Lord out of the tomb, and *we* don't know where they've put him!" (John 20:2, emphasis added), indicating that she was not the only one who was present. It is also possible that Mary Magdalene was the first to arrive at the tomb, which is why John just includes her name.

Nevertheless, these accounts all make the same point: that it was women who first saw the empty tomb and testified to the disciples about the risen Christ.

3. The Number of Angels

A third difference between the resurrection accounts is the number of angels at the empty tomb. Matthew notes one angel (Matthew 1:2–4). Mark describes "a young man dressed in a white robe" (Mark 16:5). Similarly, Luke describes two men in "dazzling clothes" (Luke 24:4), and John specifically notes two angels (John 20:12). The difference between the Gospels in this regard is likely similar to the difference between the number of the women at the tomb. Just because Matthew and Mark wrote about one angel does not mean that there weren't two.

There also seems to be a difference between the location of the angels. Mark, Luke, and John all write that the women saw the angels inside the tomb. Matthew, however, writes that an angel of the Lord rolled back the stone and was "sitting on it" (Matthew 28:2). A possible solution is that Matthew was speaking about the actions of one of the angels before the women arrived at the tomb: An angel rolled the stone away and sat on it, which caused the guards to become paralyzed with fear. Then, when the women approached and went into the tomb, they saw the angels inside of it.

All of these differences teach us that each of the Gospel writers varied their word choice. But varying one's word choice does not make the story any less true. Just as a story you and your friends shared would remain true even if you chose to tell it slightly differently, the story the Gospel writers were telling remains true, even with varying details. What matters most is the major event that each writer was writing about—the resurrection. Because each writer was faithful to that main event, we can read the differences without allowing them to take away from the truth that Jesus rose from the grave.

Application

Instead of narrowing our gaze to the minor differences we see in the Gospel accounts, we can marvel at the fact that we have four accounts written by four different men about the resurrection. Receiving one account would still have been incredible. But God, in His wisdom, used the inspiration of the Spirit to give us four accounts of the resurrection. These accounts give us proof that Jesus rose from the dead, as these accounts come from real manuscripts written by real people.

In response to these accounts, we can praise the Lord for providing us proof of Christ's resurrection. And if we ever have doubts over the validity of Christ's resurrection, we can come back to these texts and appreciate the ways in which these accounts work together to tell the same wondrous story.

QUESTION 16

What proof is there for Jesus's resurrection?

ANSWER:

The empty tomb, the hundreds of witnesses to Jesus's resurrection, and historical records speaking about Jesus and the resurrection all attest to the truth that Jesus rose from the dead.

RELEVANT PASSAGES:

Matthew 28
Luke 24
John 20–21:14
Acts 1:1–3
1 Corinthians 15:1–8

ost people — and many historians and scholars — admit that Jesus was a real person and that He did, in fact, die on the cross. However, for many, belief in who Jesus is stops there. The idea that Jesus rose from the dead is deemed preposterous, and that is one reason why people often reject Christianity.

But as believers, we know that Christ's resurrection is, in fact, true. Both God's Word as well as historical evidence confirm this truth for us. Throughout this chapter, we will look at multiple pieces of evidence from Scripture and from history that prove Jesus's resurrection. In doing so, we will be encouraged by the validity of our faith and inspired to share our faith with others — even those who might otherwise view Christ's resurrection as impossible or unreasonable.

Scriptural Evidence

1. The Empty Tomb

One of the strong pieces of evidence for Christ's resurrection is the empty tomb. When Jesus was laid in a tomb after His death, everyone expected His body to stay there. But three days later, Jesus's tomb was empty, and His body was gone.

Scripture shows us the Jewish leaders' response to the empty tomb. In Matthew 28:11–15, some of the guards assigned to Jesus's tomb approach the chief priests and report the news of the empty tomb to them. The priests decide to pay the soldiers to say, "His disciples came during the night and stole him while we were sleeping" (Matthew 28:13). Matthew goes on to explain that the guards agreed, and "this story has been spread among Jewish people to this day" (Matthew 28:15). This account shows that the Jewish leaders themselves acknowledged the empty tomb, even if they denied Christ's resurrection.

2. The Women at the Empty Tomb

Further evidence for Christ's resurrection comes from the women who discovered it. In Luke 24, women go to the tomb to finish preparing Jesus's body for burial when they discover that the tomb is empty. They then meet two angels, who confirm that Jesus has risen. Luke goes on to write, "Returning from the tomb, they reported all these things to the Eleven and to all the rest. Mary Magdalene, Joanna, Mary the mother of James, and the other women with them were telling the apostles these things" (Luke 24:9–10).

What makes this testimony so noteworthy is that it comes from women. In the first century, women were regarded as so unreliable that they were not permitted to testify in court. If Jesus's resurrection was a lie, the early Christians certainly would not have created a story in which women were the first witnesses to the empty tomb because nobody would have believed them. Thus, the fact that all four Gospel writers assert that women were the first to encounter the resurrected Jesus actually strengthens their claims. The women's testimony holds strong evidence that Jesus did, in fact, rise from the dead.

3. The Linen Wrappings Left Behind

In John 20:4–7, we learn that Jesus's linen burial wrappings were left in Jesus's tomb. This, too, is evidence for Jesus's resurrection. It is one thing for the tomb to have been opened and the grave to be empty, but it is another for Jesus's linens to be left inside. Grave robbers were common during this time in history, but if grave robbers had stolen Jesus's body, they would have kept the linens wrapped around His body, as the spices on Jesus's linens were valuable. The position of the clothes left in the tomb also attests to Jesus's resurrection, as the head wrapping was not cast aside but neatly folded (John 20:7). It is unlikely that the grave robbers felt that they ought to tidy up before they left!

4. Christ's Resurrected Appearances

Another piece of biblical evidence for Christ's resurrection is His appearances. The Gospels record Jesus's appearances to the women at the tomb and to His disciples. But Paul also writes in 1 Corinthians 15:6 that Jesus appeared to "over five hundred brothers and sisters at one time." Most of these witnesses were still alive at the time Paul wrote this letter to the Corinthians, which means that people could have asked these witnesses about their experiences and heard their testimony of the risen Christ. Paul also writes that Jesus appeared to James, the apostles, and also himself (1 Corinthians 15:7–8). Therefore, the Gospel accounts, as well as Paul's words, confirm that hundreds of eyes beheld Jesus after His death, verifying His resurrection.

Historical Evidence

While Scripture gives us ample proof of Christ's resurrection, we can also consider historical evidence. Consider the following three points.

1. The Apostles' Testimony and Willingness to Be Martyred

All of the people who saw the resurrected Christ had their own testimonies to share about Christ's resurrection — and what is particularly noteworthy is that they were willing to die for these testimonies. Many of the apostles were persecuted severely for their belief that Jesus was the Son of God who died and was raised from the dead. Apostles such as James, Peter, and Paul were even executed for their testimonies. Few people are willing to lay their lives down for their dearly held beliefs; who, then, dies for something they are uncertain of? The apostles' willingness to risk their lives for their faith shows that they were certain that Jesus is who He said He is and that they were unwavering in their testimonies about their encounters with the risen Jesus.

2. The Spread of Christianity

A belief in resurrection was unpopular during Jesus's time. For the Greeks, resurrection would have been viewed as undesirable, for they believed the goal was to escape one's body. Jews believed resurrection would happen but not until the very end of history. That said, it is incredible that the message of Christ's resurrection gained traction, leading to the spread of Christianity. The momentum and widespread reach of the Christian movement show that many people genuinely believed the testimony of those who witnessed the resurrected Christ, despite the rejection they would face due to their belief in a resurrection.

If Jesus did not rise from the dead, Christianity would not have sparked or spread in the way that it did. But Christianity did spread as believers preached a true gospel that proclaimed the life, death, and resurrection of Jesus Christ.

What is especially significant about this spread is that it occurred weeks after Jesus's death and resurrection in the very place where Jesus's death and resurrection took place. Imagine this: Jerusalem had just been shaken up by tension between believers in Jesus and those who put Him to death. But just three days after Jesus's death, there are reports circulating that He is risen. Surely these claims could have been debunked rather quickly, spreading no further than to Jesus's disciples. But not only were more and more people convinced of Jesus's resurrection, but also belief in Him spread rapidly despite the persecution Jews would face for professing faith in Jesus. The news of Jesus's resurrection did not fade away or prove false; instead, it spread, as Jesus said in Acts 1:8, "in Jerusalem, in Judea and Samaria, and to the ends of the earth."

3. Extrabiblical Writings

In addition to the testimonies of believers, we also have multiple historical records that speak about the death of Jesus as well as His disciples' response to His death. The first-century Jewish historian Josephus wrote that after Jesus died, "he appeared to [the disciples] alive again the third day, as the divine prophets had foretold these and ten thousand other wonderful things concerning him; and the tribe of Christians, so named from him, are not extinct at this day."[52] While Josephus was not a believer, his words confirm that Jesus's disciples believed He had appeared to them and also speak to the rise of Christianity in the first century.

Similarly, Pliny the Younger, Roman governor of Bithynia, wrote about the spread of Christianity. In a letter to the Roman Emperor Trajan about how to go about prosecuting the growing population of Christians, he wrote:

> Many persons of all ages, and of both sexes alike, are being brought into peril of their lives by their accusers, and the process will go on. For the contagion of this superstition has

---

52   Flavius Josephus, "Antiquities of the Jews," book 18, chap. 3.

spread not only through the free cities, but into the villages and the rural districts, and yet it seems to me that it can be checked and set right.[53]

Additionally, Suetonius, a historian and friend of Pliny the Younger, wrote: "Since the Jews constantly made disturbances at the instigation of Chrestus, [Emperor Claudius] expelled them from Rome."[54] In this quote, "Chrestus" is believed to be a misspelling of the Greek word for "Christ." Thus, Suetonius is recounting the persecution early Christians faced at the hands of Rome.

While neither Pliny the Younger nor Suetonius speak specifically about Christ's resurrection, they do speak to the very real response to it — the growing traction of Christianity by those who believed in the risen Savior.

Application

The truth of Christ's resurrection is the foundation of the Christian faith. As believers, we have confidence that Christ's resurrection is not something we hope is true but something we know is true. And because we know Christ's resurrection is true, we are all the more motivated to share the gospel with others.

Just as many of Jesus's witnesses shared their testimony about the risen Savior with others, so also are we able to share with others our own testimony of Christ's salvation and the truth of His life, death, and resurrection. We can also share the proof of Christ's resurrection with those who are skeptical of Christianity. While there are wonderful examples from Scripture we can point to, we can also share corroborating accounts and evidence from history, as many don't know that Jesus was written about in sources other than the Bible. Yet

---

53 Pliny the Younger, *Letters of Pliny the Younger*, book 10, letters 1–60.

54 Gaius Suetonius Tranquillus, "Life of Claudius."

both God's Word and historical records prove and defend the truth that Jesus is alive.

It is important to note that we've only scratched the surface of evidence for Christ's resurrection in this chapter—there is certainly more evidence one could point to. So, if this is a topic that interests you, we encourage you to do your own investigation and then share your findings with others as a way to encourage them to put their hope in Jesus, our Savior who is truly alive.

QUESTION 17

Why is Jesus's resurrection significant for us?

_____

ANSWER:

Jesus's resurrection confirms that His work of salvation is complete and secures both our spiritual and physical resurrection.

RELEVANT PASSAGES:

Acts 2:24
Romans 4:25, 6:4–5
1 Corinthians 15
Philippians 3:20–21

elievers often find themselves asking this question at some point in their lives: How do I know that I am truly saved? We crave the assurance that our salvation is real and secure. Praise be to God that we can look to Jesus's resurrection and find the assurance we so desire!

When we reflect on the truth of Christ's resurrection, we are reminded of its significance in two ways: It confirms that His work is complete, and it secures our own resurrection to come. Let's look at each a little more closely to understand what Christ's resurrection means for us and the hope, security, and assurance it provides.

1. Jesus's Work of Salvation Is Complete

When Jesus rose from the dead, He declared that He conquered both sin and death. If Christ did not rise from the dead, we would still be in our sins (1 Corinthians 15:16–19). We would still be guilty for our sin and therefore still deserve punishment for our sin. But, as we discussed in the previous chapter, we can have confidence that Jesus has risen. He has paid the price for our sin on the cross and offered us forgiveness. We have been justified, made right with God through the righteousness we have been given through Christ. As Paul proclaims, "He was delivered up for our trespasses and raised for our justification" (Romans 4:25). Because Christ's work is now complete, we can rest in all He's done for us, recognizing that there is nothing more we could do to add to our salvation.

2. Our Resurrection Is Secured

Jesus's resurrection also has incredible implications for our own resurrection. The salvation we receive from Jesus makes us new and assures us that we will be raised to live with Christ one day. In Him, we experience both spiritual resurrection (which we have already received) and physical resurrection (which we will one day receive when He returns). In both, we experience freedom in the present and hope for the future.

Spiritual Resurrection

First, Jesus's resurrection secures our spiritual resurrection. This is often referred to as regeneration, or our being born again and made new. Because of Christ's resurrection, those of us who have placed our faith in Christ have been brought from death to life. We have been cleansed and made new. Through Christ's salvation and the regeneration we receive as a result, we receive a spiritual resurrection. We are no longer who we once were before coming to Christ; we now walk in the new life we have received through Christ's salvation. Paul speaks to this truth in Romans 6:4–5 when he writes:

> Therefore we were buried with him by baptism into death, in order that, just as Christ was raised from the dead by the glory of the Father, so we too may walk in newness of life. For if we have been united with him in the likeness of his death, we will certainly also be in the likeness of his resurrection.

Because of our spiritual resurrection, we are no longer captive to our sin but instead live in freedom from our sin. Jesus's victory over sin and death secures our own victory, which means that we are victorious over our sin and able to fight against our sin through the power of the Holy Spirit. Because of our spiritual resurrection, we are also no longer separated from God but brought into a relationship with Him. And we are united with Christ — tethered to Him for eternity — and receive all the spiritual blessings that come with our union with Him. If we are in Christ, we are living out all the blessings of our resurrection life right here and now.

Physical Resurrection

But there is one aspect of our resurrection life that is still yet to come. While we have received a spiritual resurrection through Christ, we will also one day receive a physical resurrection. Because Jesus conquered death, we have hope that we, too, will conquer death (1 Corinthians 15:54–55). If we are in Christ, we are promised that after we die, we will be raised to eternal life with Christ. Just as death was not the end for Jesus, death will not be the end for those in Christ. However, it is not just our souls that will be with God after death. Scripture tells us that believers will experience a physical resurrection when Jesus returns to set all things right.

Though Jesus has washed our sins away, we continue to live in bodies that are broken by sin. Our hearts may be restored, yet our bodies still need to be restored. But God's plan for restoration involves our bodies, and He has promised us that we will receive this restoration. Paul confirms this promise in Philippians 3:20–21 by saying:

> Our citizenship is in heaven, and we eagerly wait for a Savior from there, the Lord Jesus Christ. He will transform the body of our humble condition into the likeness of his glorious body, by the power that enables him to subject everything to himself.

Jesus's physical resurrection confirms our own physical resurrection. Paul writes in 1 Corinthians 15:20–21, "But as it is, Christ has been raised from the dead, the firstfruits of those who have fallen asleep. For since death came through a man, the resurrection of the dead also comes through a man." The firstfruits of a harvest would determine what the rest of the harvest would be like. In a similar way, because Christ has been raised from the dead, we know that we will also be raised from the dead. We will receive new, resurrected bodies that will not be tainted by sin. Paul describes this truth when he writes, "For the trumpet will sound, and the dead will be raised incorruptible, and we will be changed" (1 Corinthians 15:52b). As followers of Jesus, we live with hope that because of our resurrected Savior, we will one day know what it's like to live in bodies that are completely perfected.

Application

Jesus's resurrection assures us that the salvation we have received by grace through faith is secure. Therefore, when we find ourselves doubting our salvation or questioning who Jesus is, we can look to the resurrection and be reminded that Jesus is the King of kings who conquered death so that we would never taste death.

As we rest in the truth of the resurrection, we are encouraged to look ahead to the resurrection to come. Looking to our future resurrection gives us hope in the present because we know that the broken bodies we live in will one day be made new. Our future resurrection also brings purpose to our present. Paul tells us that in light of our hope of resurrection and our sure victory in Jesus, we can excel in the Lord's work, knowing that our "labor in the Lord is not in vain" (1 Corinthians 15:58).

Because we belong to God's kingdom and will live in God's kingdom forever, we know that what we do for the Lord on this side of eternity matters. Let's fix our eyes on the hope ahead and allow our future to impact our present as we work joyfully for the Lord.

PART III
JESUS'S ASCENSION

*Jesus's ascension reminds us
that Jesus is alive, reigning
over heaven and earth.*

Introduction to

Part III

JESUS'S ASCENSION

art II of this book covered Jesus's miraculous resurrection from the dead. For forty days after His resurrection, He taught the disciples, performed miracles, and explained how He was the fulfillment of all Scripture. On His final day with the disciples, Jesus gathered them all together and gave them His final instruction. When He finished, the disciples asked Him, "Lord, are you restoring the kingdom to Israel at this time?" (Acts 1:6).

He responded, "It is not for you to know times or periods that the Father has set by his own authority. But you will receive power when the Holy Spirit has come on you, and you will be my witnesses in Jerusalem, in all Judea and Samaria, and to the ends of the earth" (Acts 1:7–8).

No one could have expected what happened next. Right before their eyes, He ascended. He was raised to heaven, lifted higher and higher until the clouds blocked Him from sight. Then, two men appeared where Jesus had once been.

The two men said to the onlookers, "Men of Galilee, why do you stand looking up into heaven? This same Jesus, who has been taken from you into heaven, will come in the same way that you have seen him going into heaven" (Acts 1:11).

Little did the disciples know that their question about restoring the kingdom had anticipated Jesus's work in His ascension. Instead of restoring the kingdom of Israel, He would be establishing and fulfilling the kingdom of heaven. And He has invited all of God's people to partake in the glorious reign of His kingdom.

In this section, we will see how Jesus's ascension teaches us more about where Jesus is now, what He is currently doing, and what this means for our lives as Christians. Ultimately, Jesus's ascension reminds us that Jesus is alive, reigning over heaven and earth, and that He has paved a way for us to join Him in heaven one day.

Question 18

Where is Jesus now, and what is He doing?

_____

Answer:

Jesus is currently seated at the right hand of the Father, sustaining creation, caring for His Church, and preparing a future home for His people.

Relevant Passages:

John 14:1–3, 15:1–7
Romans 8:34
Colossians 1:17–18
Ephesians 4:11–13, 5:23–27
Hebrews 7:25

ave you ever stopped and looked up at the sky? Maybe you have stood outside at night, staring up at the stars. Or maybe you've watched the clouds turn various shades of pink and orange as the sun traded places with the moon. In Acts 1:9, as the disciples looked up into the sky, they got the opportunity to witness something truly unique: Christ's ascension.

Luke records the ascension in this way, "And while he was blessing them, he left them and was carried up into heaven" (Luke 24:51). Similarly, in Acts 1:9–11, Luke writes:

> After he had said this, he was taken up as they were watching, and a cloud took him out of their sight. While he was going, they were gazing into heaven, and suddenly two men in white clothes stood by them. They said, "Men of Galilee, why do you stand looking up into heaven? This same Jesus, who has been taken from you into heaven, will come in the same way that you have seen him going into heaven."

Christ had spent forty days on earth, but then, with His ascension, He was taken up in glory into heaven from among the presence of the apostles. Where is our ascended Christ now? He remains in heaven, exalted and seated at the right hand of God the Father (Acts 2:33, 7:55–56; 1 Timothy 3:16; Hebrews 1:3).

However, this leads us to a natural next question: What is Christ currently *doing* from His place of honor and glory in heaven? When we ask this question, we are considering Christ's *session*, a theological term often used in conjunction with the work that Christ continues to do from heaven.

When He took His seat next to the Father, Jesus received rule, authority, glory, honor, power, and dominion (Ephesians 1:20–21, 1 Peter 3:22), and He is now currently exercising this power to reign over and serve His people until He returns.

Specifically, we can see Christ's present work at the right hand of God in several ways: He sustains creation, He cares for His Church, and He prepares a heavenly home for believers.

Christ's Present Work to Sustain Creation

In Colossians 1:16–17, Paul tells us that "all things have been created through [Christ] and for him" and "by him all things hold together." Without Christ's work of creation, nothing would exist, and without His work of sustaining, creation would cease to be. Job says, "If he put his mind to it and withdrew the spirit and breath he gave, every living thing would perish together and mankind would return to the dust" (Job 34:14–15). All of creation exists and serves its God-given purpose because Jesus sustains it. Without Jesus, electrons don't circle, gravity doesn't hold things to the ground, planets don't orbit, cells don't reproduce, the sun doesn't shine, rain doesn't fall from the clouds, and our hearts don't beat. All things are upheld by the power of Christ.

Christ's Present Work to Care for His Church

While Christ sustains all of creation, the Word also specifically details some of the ways He sustains His people, the Church. Let's examine a few of the different ways He does so.

Christ Cares for His Church by Leading, Nurturing, and Cleansing It

After discussing Christ's power in creating and sustaining the world, Paul continues in Colossians 1 by declaring that Christ "is the head of the body, the church" (Colossians 1:18). Christ's headship of the Church can be summarized as His ruling over and nurturing of the Church. He rules over the Church through His Spirit and His Word. His Word declares His will to His people, instructing them how to live for His glory, and His Spirit applies those truths to their lives.

As the head of the body, He is also the source of life for the Church. Jesus Himself says in the Gospel of Matthew that He will build His Church, and the gates of hell will not prevail against it (Matthew 16:18). Nothing can separate the Church from the loving care of Jesus. Ephesians 5:29 tells us that Christ provides and cares for the body because of His love for her. One of the ways He does this is by cleansing the Church and judging sin (Ephesians 5:25–27; Revelation 2:5, 16).

God has always been concerned with the purity and holiness of His people. When the Israelites were about to enter into the Promised Land, He instructed them to drive out those people who lived sinful lifestyles so that they, too, wouldn't fall into lives of sin (Numbers 33:52; see also Exodus 23:29, Leviticus 18:24). Similarly, Christ cleanses His Church of people who refuse to turn from their wicked ways. By removing those who persist in sin and refuse to accept His grace, Jesus protects the rest of His flock from temptation that might arise from within the body (Matthew 16:6–12, 1 Corinthians 5:6–8).

Similarly, when Jesus's Church goes through the steps of restoration for an individual who has sinned and that individual insists on persisting in sin instead of repenting, Jesus promises to be with His people in a special way (Matthew 18:15–20). Through His presence, He is sustaining a church in what is often one of the most difficult things they can walk through.

Christ Cares for His Church by Serving It

In addition to sustaining His Church, Jesus also selflessly serves His Church. For example, there are two blessings Christ bestows upon believers at the moment of their conversion. First, He baptizes His people in the Holy Spirit (John 1:33; see also Acts 1:5, 11:16, and John 20:22). From that moment on, they are permanently indwelt by the Holy Spirit and enabled by His power to say "no" to sin and "yes" to Christ. Second, Christ also gives at least one spiritual gift to each and every person who believes in Him (Romans 12:4–8, 1 Corinthians 12:18–28, Ephesians 4:11–13). These gifts are then exercised in the Church so that the body is built up into the likeness of Christ. But this maturing of the body isn't done solely through the work of spiritual gifts. Christ Himself gives grace to believers (Ephesians 4:7), strengthens them (Philippians 4:13), protects them (2 Thessalonians 3:3), and produces spiritual fruit in their lives (John 15:4–5).

However, Jesus's ministry to and on behalf of His body isn't limited to their physical lives here on earth; it extends to heaven as well. Romans 8:34 and Hebrews 7:25 tell us that Jesus is currently sitting at the right hand of God interceding and advocating for His people. No one can bring a charge before God against His elect (Romans 8:33) because God has justified those in Christ, and Christ intercedes on their behalf.

Christ's Present Work to Prepare a Place for Us

Finally, for those of us in Christ, there is great hope for the future. For while we are eagerly awaiting His return, Christ is preparing a heavenly home for us that we will enjoy with Him forever (John 14:1–3, Revelation 21:1–4).

Application

Christ is not a distant deity or an uninvolved God. He didn't just create the world and step back to watch it spin. He is actively involved in His creation and His Church. He is caring and close.

Colossians 1:27 tells us of "the mystery that is Christ in you, the hope of glory" (NASB). When you are struggling with God or the problems and pain of life, remember that Christ is never far away. He is in you, sustaining you and working in your life to make you more like Himself (Philippians 1:6). Despite what is leaving you weary and burdened, you can come to Him, and He will give you rest for your soul. So let the One who sustains share His yoke with you, for it is comfortable and light (Matthew 11:28–30, NASB).

How does the Old Testament point to Jesus's death, resurrection, and ascension?

ANSWER:

All of Scripture points to Jesus Christ, and there are multiple prophecies and allusions from hundreds and thousands of years before His death, resurrection, and ascension that miraculously foretell these events.

RELEVANT PASSAGES:

Psalm 16:8–11, 22:1–18, 68, 110
Isaiah 53
Jeremiah 19:1
Hosea 6:1–3
Jonah 1:17
Zechariah 11:13

The same day that Jesus rose from the dead, two disciples walked and talked about everything that had just taken place over the past couple of days. Then, Jesus joined them on their journey to a village called Emmaus. At the time, the disciples were prevented from recognizing that the man walking alongside them was indeed Jesus Christ — their Rabbi for the past three years who had been crucified mere days before.

After the disciples had finished detailing the events of the past few days, it was then Jesus's turn to speak. As He did so, He went all the way back to the Old Testament and "interpreted for them the things concerning himself in all the Scriptures" (Luke 24:27). This verse reminds us that everything in Scripture points to Jesus — everything points to God's plan to save His people through the death and resurrection of Christ.

If Jesus confirms that all of Scripture prophesies about Him, then let's take a closer look at some of the specific prophecies that foretold Jesus's death, resurrection, and ascension. This certainly isn't an exhaustive list; however, it will give us, as readers, an overview of how the Old Testament points to the work Jesus came to do.

Prophecies About Jesus's Death

The Suffering Servant — Isaiah 53

Isaiah 53 is one of the most well-known Old Testament passages concerning the death of Jesus Christ. Isaiah 53 describes a Servant of the Lord who would suffer cruelty at the hands of His people. Yet despite the suffering and pain He would endure, He would still bear the guilt and shame of the very people who would condemn Him.

The prophecy begins by explaining the Servant's lowliness and humble origins and that He would be rejected by His own people and nation (Isaiah 53:3). Then, the prophecy continues in Isaiah 53:4–6 by detailing the pain — both physical and spiritual — that the Servant would bear on behalf of sinful people. But through His suffering, God's people would receive salvation because of the Servant's faithfulness.

In Isaiah 53:7–9, the prophecy gives more specific details about the occurrences surrounding the Servant's death. Isaiah begins by saying this suffering Servant would remain silent before His accusers. He would be like a lamb led to the slaughter. Matthew 26:63 and 27:12–14, as well as Mark 14:60–61 and 15:4–5, all attest to Jesus's silence during the false accusations of the chief priests, elders, and Pilate.

Finally, Isaiah 53:9 describes the suffering Servant who wouldn't even have His own grave to be buried in. His grave would belong to a rich man, who would take pity on the suffering Servant because of the cruel and unfair death that He endured. This would be fulfilled in Matthew 27:57–60 when a rich man from Arimathea named Joseph took Jesus's body and buried Him in Joseph's tomb.

The Betrayal — Zechariah 11:13 and Various Passages from Jeremiah

Matthew 27:3–10 describes the aftermath of Judas Iscariot's betrayal of Jesus. In this narrative, Judas feels remorse for his sin and betrayal and tries to return the money that the chief priests and elders paid him, but they refuse since his money is now considered "blood money" (Matthew 27:6). Judas then hangs himself, and the chief priests and elders use the returned money to purchase a potter's field, called "Field of Blood," which was a burial place for foreigners.

In recording this narrative, Matthew seems to see a connection to several Old Testament passages and themes. To start, there is a clear connection here to Zechariah 11:13, in which the Lord tells the prophet Zechariah, "Throw it to the potter." Zechariah then clarifies that this command from the Lord refers to the "price I was valued by them." And then he writes, "So I took the thirty pieces of silver and threw it into the house of the LORD, to the potter."

There also seems to be a connection to various passages in Jeremiah that speak of a potter (Jeremiah 18–19) and describe Jeremiah's purchase of a piece of land (Jeremiah 32), though commentators have differing thoughts on what specific passage(s) in Jeremiah that Matthew has in mind. Nevertheless, there is definitely a strong Old Testament connection at work in this story of Judas Iscariot.

The Cross—Psalm 22

In the Gospels of Matthew and Mark, Jesus quotes from Psalm 22, a psalm that prophesies His death on the cross. Quoting the first verse of this psalm as He dies on the cross, Jesus cries out with a loud voice, "My God, my God, why have you abandoned me?" (Matthew 27:46, Mark 15:34).

Psalm 22 begins with the psalmist, David, crying out to God, who feels far away. To David, it feels like God has abandoned him. But as the psalm continues, his cries of anguish are turned into songs of praise as he remembers the Lord's eternal promises: Those who are humbled will be blessed by the Lord, and the rulers and kingdoms of all empires will eventually bow down to the Almighty God. David concludes this psalm by saying that through the works of God's righteousness, generations of people who have yet to be born will declare the Lord's goodness forever. Therefore, Jesus's reference to Psalm 22:1 while on the cross draws attention not only to the wrath poured out on Him but also to the hope of His kingdom to come.

Additionally, Psalm 22:18 says, "They divided my garments among themselves, and they cast lots for my clothing." This would be recorded in the Gospels of Matthew, Luke, and John as the soldiers at the foot of the cross divided Jesus's garments among themselves by casting lots.

Prophecies About Jesus's Resurrection

The Third Day — Jonah 1:17 and Hosea 6:1–3

There are a couple of Old Testament stories that allude to or foreshadow the resurrection of Jesus Christ occurring on the third day. The first is the story of Jonah. In this Old Testament book, the prophet Jonah — who was attempting to run away from the Lord — was swallowed by a great fish. Jonah 1:17 says that Jonah remained in the belly of the fish for three days and three nights. Then, on the third day, the Lord commanded the fish to vomit Jonah onto dry land. This story foreshadows the three days that Jesus spent in the grave before being raised back to life (Matthew 12:40).

The second is Hosea 6:1–3. These verses call for the people of Israel to repent of their sins and disobedience. They describe how the Lord will eventually use the people's suffering to heal them if they turn back to the Lord. In Hosea 6:2, Hosea writes, "He will revive us after two days, and on the third day he will raise us up so we can live in his presence." Although Hosea is addressing God's people in his current day, his words still foreshadow Jesus's resurrection. All Christians are united to Jesus through His resurrection. He has joined all of us to Himself, and therefore, we get to enjoy the benefit of His resurrection, which is eternal life.

The Empty Tomb — Psalm 16:8–11

When the Holy Spirit came upon the disciples during Pentecost, the Apostle Peter stood up among the crowds and boldly proclaimed the gospel of Jesus Christ to all who listened. During his speech, he explained how Jesus Christ lived a sinless life, performed great signs and miracles, and was crucified on the cross. But Acts 2:24 says, "God raised him up, ending the pains of death, because it was not possible for him to be held by death." Then, Peter points to Psalm 16:8–11 as the fulfillment of this prophecy. In the psalm, the author confidently affirms that God will not abandon the psalmist in Sheol, nor will He let His "faithful one" see decay (Psalm 16:10). Peter goes on to explain that the psalm does not refer to King David because he has remained both dead and buried (Acts 2:29), but the psalm prophesies about the One who would defeat death and would never decay in a tomb, which is Jesus Christ.

Prophecies About Jesus's Ascension

The Exaltation of Christ — Psalm 110

Psalm 110 is the most frequently quoted psalm in all the New Testament writings. It describes Jesus's unique role as a priest who will come from the line of Melchizedek (Psalm 110:4), Jesus's defeat of His enemies (Psalm 110:2), and Jesus's exaltation in heaven (Psalm 110:1). In Acts 2:33–36, Peter concluded his sermon on the day of Pentecost by telling the people how Jesus Christ fulfilled the prophecy of Psalm 110:1. Jesus ascended to heaven, and He was exalted to sit at the right hand of God. This is a sign of Jesus's authority and power over all, and it is fulfilled by His ascension into heaven.

The Gifts of Christ — Psalm 68

In Ephesians 4:7–8, the Apostle Paul explains to the Ephesian church members how Jesus equips all people in the church with unique gifts and talents in order to build one another up in spiritual maturity and growth. In Paul's defense for each member's unique role in the church body, he explains how Christ's ascension is the means by which Christ is able to give gifts to His people through the power of the Holy Spirit. And Paul uses Psalm 68:18 to confirm this stance.

Psalm 68 is a psalm that celebrates God's protection over His people and His presence that dwelt in the ark of the covenant. The psalmist celebrates God's victory over His enemies, and Psalm 68:18 speaks of God being exalted over His people, an exaltation that is ultimately fulfilled thousands of years later when the risen Jesus would ascend to heaven. The psalm prophesies that when this One ascends into heaven, it will be the means by which the Lord God will dwell with His people once again. Jesus Christ fulfilled this prophecy as He ascended into heaven, allowing the gift of the Holy Spirit to descend upon His people in order for God's presence to dwell in the very hearts of Christians.

Application

Indeed, all of Scripture points to the death, resurrection, and ascension of Jesus Christ. Led by the Spirit of God, the authors of Old Testament Scripture from thousands of years before Christ's birth foretold God's plan to save His people through the work of our Savior, Jesus Christ.

The many prophecies throughout Scripture that point to Jesus's death, resurrection, and ascension affirm that the authors of Scripture were miraculously led by the Spirit of God. We can trust that when we read and study Scripture—both Old and New Testaments—it leads us to fully love and understand Jesus Christ in a deeper way.

QUESTION 20

Why is Jesus's ascension significant for us?

ANSWER:

Because Jesus physically ascended into heaven, we can have sure confidence that He is ruling and reigning over all creation and that He will physically return one day to restore all things. As those who trust in His life, death, and resurrection, we can look toward this day with hope.

RELEVANT PASSAGES:

John 14:2–3
Acts 1:6–11
Romans 8:34
Colossians 3:1
1 Thessalonians 4:16–18
Hebrews 4:14–16
1 Peter 3:22
Revelation 3:21

our alarm clock goes off in the morning. Lazily, you peek one eye open. One by one, you stretch out all your stiff and sore arms and legs. Even as your body is still waking up, your brain is already running one hundred miles per hour. You remember the work you have to finish today, the time you *don't* have to finish all of it, and the fear and anxiety that kept you awake the night before.

In these moments when life feels suffocating, your first instinct is probably not to consider the ascension of Jesus Christ. In fact, most of us likely spend very little of our days contemplating this critical aspect of Jesus's ministry on earth. But despite our lack of thoughtfulness about Jesus's ascension, it has incredible implications for our daily lives.

Jesus's ascension is the guarantee that our Savior is reigning and ruling at the right hand of God in heaven (1 Peter 3:22). His ascension proves that He has ultimate authority over all the universe, both heaven and earth. It promises that He will physically return one day to restore all of His creation and that He has invited God's people to participate in His eternal life.

When Jesus came to earth, He lived a perfect life, died on a cross, rose from the dead, and ascended into heaven. Without the last proclamation that Christ ascended, we would miss a critical aspect of Jesus's divinity and authority over all creation. Therefore, in this chapter, we will look at three ways Jesus's ascension is significant for our everyday lives.

The first reason Jesus's ascension is significant for our lives today is that it brings us the comforting reminder that Christ is King over all creation. He is not only alive, as the resurrection proves, but in His physical, ascended body, He is also actively ruling and reigning over all things at the right hand of God. Jesus has been given authority over all creation, and He reigns as King. Thus, His ascension is the bridge that connects His lordship over earth and heaven. There is nothing done in either heaven or on earth that goes beyond His lordship, His power, His knowledge, His sovereignty, or His authority. He reigns on the highest throne with the utmost authority.

Therefore, when we face overwhelming anxieties, when we don't have the strength to get out of bed in the morning, when life feels like one disappointment after another, we can remember that the Lord over our lives is actively ruling and reigning over all. We can remember that He is powerfully sovereign over every minute of our lives. We can remember that He is present with us, no matter what we are facing. And we can remember that He is coming again.

This brings us to the second reason Jesus's ascension is significant: It guarantees that He will return for His people and restore His creation for good. He is currently reigning over heaven and earth, but one day, He will return to earth to restore all things. In Acts 1:10–11, two men appeared to the disciples after Christ's resurrection, telling them that Jesus will return to earth from heaven in the same way the disciples saw Him go into heaven from earth. He will not return to earth as a baby wrapped in swaddling cloths as He did when He was incarnated (Luke 2:12). This time, He will come down from heaven as the victorious, all-powerful King of kings and Lord of lords (Revelation 19:16). He will conquer Satan once and for all, and He will establish a new heaven and a new earth for His people to enter into forevermore.

And the overarching gift that we get to enjoy in Jesus Christ's ascension is this: We are invited to partake in it all. The final reason Jesus's ascension is significant is that we can look forward to the day when we will get to enjoy His presence for all eternity. When we accepted Christ's salvation, we were not only united to His presence through the Holy Spirit; we were also united to all His future promises through His ascension. As the King of heaven and earth, He has paved a way for us to enter into His kingdom. We get to have joy in the hope that we are citizens of heaven and that He has prepared a place for us there (John 14:2–3).

Application

When we feel like no one sees our hurt and our pain, we can know that Christ is alive and active in our life. When we feel overwhelmed by our circumstances, we can find comfort in our Savior who is sovereign over everything in all of creation. When we feel the grief of this world's brokenness, we can remember that our hope for a new heaven and new earth is secure in Jesus Christ.

Our citizenship is bound to Jesus Christ, and His ascension guarantees that we will physically be present with Him one day. Therefore, even as we still live in our present-day world, bodies, and circumstances, we set our minds on things above (Colossians 3:2). We look to Jesus Christ and rearrange our lives under His lordship. We place our hope not in things of this world but in our ascended Savior, who is fully alive and reigns over all creation forever.

QUESTION 21

Jesus defeated death and then ascended. Shouldn't my suffering be over?

ANSWER:

Unfortunately, we still experience pain and suffering even though Jesus defeated death. This idea is best understood according to the reality that we live between the first and second comings of Christ. Yes, Jesus paid it all on the cross, but the effects of sin (e.g., suffering) will continue until He returns again.

RELEVANT PASSAGES:

John 11:25–26, 16:33
Romans 6:9
1 Corinthians 15:54–57
2 Timothy 1:10

hristians often think that life ought to be easy. Scripture talks about how God loves us, and He is for us. *Shouldn't this mean that if I do my best to obey His commandments, then difficulties, struggles, and suffering will be minimal?* Unfortunately, trusting in Christ does not guarantee a life of comfort on earth. If you talk to anyone who has walked with Jesus for even a short amount of time, they can likely detail for you the pains and struggles that accompany this faith journey.

But doesn't the Bible promise, "A man reaps what he sows" (Galatians 6:7–9, NIV) and that God does not plan to "harm you ... [but] to give you hope and a future" (Jeremiah 29:11, NIV)? When taken out of context, these verses often leave us with a misunderstanding of what Jesus actually accomplished on the cross and an overinflated view of God's promises toward us. And this reality becomes painfully obvious in the moments when we are confronted with grief.

Many of us have grieved the loss of a loved one — perhaps a parent, grandparent, sibling, or even a child. In these times of grief and suffering, many Christians often think about the verse that states, "O death, where is your sting?" (1 Corinthians 15:55, ESV). The Bible appears to communicate that death is defeated and no longer stings because of Jesus's resurrection, but the pangs of experiencing the death of our loved ones still ring true in our soul. How can this be?

When these questions flood our souls, we must remember two things: what Jesus has already accomplished on the cross and what He promises to do one day when He returns.

First, we must understand what Jesus accomplished on the cross. Scottish pastor and theologian John Murray explains it this way: "When we think of the application of redemption we must not think of it as one simple and indivisible act. It comprises a series of acts of processes. To mention some, we have calling, regeneration, justification, adoption, sanctification, [and] glorification."[55] Yes, Jesus defeated death on the cross. But what exactly does that mean?

Murray reminds us that the ramifications of the cross are vast, but in its simplest form, Jesus's death removed the penalty of sin for all who believe, which was eternal death (Romans 6:23). So, yes, death was defeated. If you die without Christ, you live an eternal life of death, that is, separation from God. But on the contrary, for those who believe, "the gift of God is eternal life" (Romans 6:23). If you remember when Jesus was breathing His last breaths on the cross (see Question 5 for more on this), He cried out, "It is finished." What, exactly, was finished? The payment for sin. Jesus is the substitutionary sacrifice for our sin.

Second, we must also remember that in God's infinite sovereignty, He saw fit for a Second Advent, or a Second Coming. And this is our tension. This is why we often don't understand why we still struggle in life, even though Jesus paid it all.

We live between the comings of Christ. Jesus came as a baby and entered Jerusalem on a humble donkey, but He will return yet again as King, riding a white horse (Revelation 19:11). Between these two stories is where we exist. It's where we live. And at times, it is

---

55 Murray, *Redemption Accomplished and Applied* (repr., William B. Eerdmans Publishing Company, 2015), 82.

where we suffer. Even though Jesus has already paid the price for our sin, He has not yet fought the final fight. Theologians refer to this time as the "already but not yet" and consider it to be a part of "inaugurated eschatology," a term that refers to events in the end times (eschatology) that began (or were inaugurated) with the life, death, and resurrection of Christ.

While the goal of this book is to primarily focus on the death, burial, resurrection, and ascension of Christ, we must also acknowledge that there is more to the story. The cross and ascension are not the bookends of Christ's work, but rather, together, they are the first bookend of this already-but-not-yet era we find ourselves in.

Application

Life is hard. It is difficult and exhausting at times. Perhaps we can all agree on that. And thankfully, Scripture offers us many verses of hope. If you find yourself grasping for hope, there is good news here. True hope is found in the person and work of Jesus.

However, there is often a cost to following Christ. We still live in a broken world because Christ has not yet established the New Jerusalem (Revelation 21:1–2). So, while we wait, we cling to the hope that He is with us.

The late David Powlison was one of our era's most beloved biblical counseling professors at Westminster Theological Seminary. When asked, *What does it mean that God will "bless" us?* Powlison replied, "In promising this God explicitly does *not* mean that he will give you mere comfort, [or] warm feelings ... [but] God is at your side."[56] The hope of the gospel in the midst of your suffering is that God is with you, even as you wait for Christ's return.

Perhaps you've recently felt the sting of death, or perhaps your life has been filled with other struggles and sorrows. At times, you may feel

---

56 Powlison, *God's Grace in Your Suffering*, 62.

that God is distant, or worse, you may convince yourself that Jesus's work on the cross was not enough for your scenario. Dear friend, that is not true. No one understands your loneliness, pain, or sorrow as well as Jesus. He was betrayed by a friend, rejected by people He loved, and murdered for a crime He did not commit. He understands your sorrow, so much so that He offered Himself as a remedy to your pain.

While your pain is not gone in totality today, cling to the One who offers hope that it will be gone one day. As our beloved Paul wrote in Romans 8:38–39, "For I am persuaded that neither death nor life, nor angels nor rulers, nor things present nor things to come, nor powers, nor height nor depth, nor any other created thing will be able to separate us from the love of God that is in Christ Jesus our Lord."

CONCLUSION

The disciples' lives would never be the same. One night, they were celebrating Passover with their Rabbi and casually enjoying each other's company like they had many nights for three years. Only a few hours later, however, their lives turned completely upside down as the Roman soldiers arrived in the garden. Then, in rapid succession, they watched Jesus be betrayed, arrested, beaten, interrogated, shamed, crucified, and buried. But even after all the miracles they had witnessed Jesus perform over the past three years, they then got to experience the most incredible miracle of all: Jesus Christ resurrected from the dead.

He remained with them for over a month—teaching them about the Scriptures and showing them all the prophecies He fulfilled. Even though Jesus stayed with them for forty days before He ascended into heaven (Acts 1:3), there were still so many questions left unanswered. So many words left unsaid. So many hopes, dreams, and plans with their Teacher that were cut short. But their response to all the changes, surprises, and life-altering events that took place in their lives in just a few weeks was not to feel discouraged that they didn't understand everything perfectly. Their response was to gather together to pray and worship God (Acts 1:9–14, Luke 24:50–52). You see, the only proper response to experiencing God is worship.

We get to experience the same thing. We get to experience Christ crucified, Christ resurrected, and Christ ascended. We have experienced how the Holy Spirit transformed us from enemies of God to children of God, and daily He conforms us into greater and greater Christlikeness. This is now the reality of our lives, but we still have so many questions left unanswered. Even as we've written this resource seeking to answer many of those questions surrounding Jesus's death, resurrection, and ascension, we must also come to terms with the reality that we will never fully understand every single detail about our Lord. But we're still invited to worship Him — because not knowing everything should actually lead us to worship Him even more.

Our God is beyond our human comprehension; we simply do not possess the capacity to fully understand His nature. Yet He still reveals Himself to us. He still gives us glimpses of who He is and what He's doing and how He's working in our everyday lives. We rest in faith that God has told us everything we need to know about Himself, and for everything else we simply cannot understand, we worship Him for being a God who is far greater than our wildest imagination.

We hope that through this book, you were able to catch a small glimpse of God's majesty through the death, resurrection, and ascension of His Son, Jesus Christ. Our goal for this book is that you walk away with more wonder and awe about our Savior. Our Lord died on the cross for our sins, rose from the dead, and ascended to the right hand of God. May this gospel truth be the foundation for every moment of your life — even the unremarkable, mundane moments. And we pray, more than anything else, that it would lead you to worship Him. So, let's continue to ask good questions. Let's continue to seek answers in the Bible. And in all things, let's continue to praise His great and glorious name now and forevermore.

Appendix A:
Verses About Christ's Substitution

But he was pierced because of our rebellion, *crushed because of our iniquities;* punishment for our peace was on him, and we are healed by his wounds.

Isaiah 53:5

For even the Son of Man did not come to be served, but to serve, and *to give his life as a ransom for many.*

Mark 10:45

I am the good shepherd. The good shepherd *lays down his life for the sheep.*

John 10:11

He was delivered up for our trespasses and raised for our justification.

Romans 4:25

For while we were still helpless, at the right time, Christ *died for the ungodly.*

Romans 5:6

But God proves his own love for us in that while we were still sinners, *Christ died for us.*

Romans 5:8

For the love of Christ compels us, since we have reached this conclusion, that *one died for all, and therefore all died.*

2 Corinthians 5:14

He made the one who did not know sin to be sin for us, so that in him we might become the righteousness of God.

2 CORINTHIANS 5:21

Grace to you and peace from God the Father and our Lord Jesus Christ, *who gave himself for our sins* to rescue us from this present evil age, according to the will of our God and Father.

GALATIANS 1:3–4

Christ redeemed us from the curse of the law *by becoming a curse for us,* because it is written, Cursed is everyone who is hung on a tree.

GALATIANS 3:13

Therefore, be imitators of God, as dearly loved children, and walk in love, as Christ also loved us and *gave himself for us,* a sacrificial and fragrant offering to God.

EPHESIANS 5:1–2

For God did not appoint us to wrath, but to obtain salvation through our Lord Jesus Christ, *who died for us,* so that whether we are awake or asleep, we may live together with him.

1 THESSALONIANS 5:9–10

For there is one God and one mediator between God and mankind, the man Christ Jesus, *who gave himself as a ransom for all,* a testimony at the proper time.

1 TIMOTHY 2:5–6

He *gave himself for us* to redeem us from all lawlessness and to cleanse for himself a people for his own possession, eager to do good works.

TITUS 2:14

And just as it is appointed for people to die once — and after this, judgment — so also *Christ, having been offered once to bear the sins of many,* will appear a second time, not to bear sin, but to bring salvation to those who are waiting for him.

HEBREWS 9:27–28

For you were called to this, because Christ also *suffered for you,* leaving you an example, that you should follow in his steps.

1 PETER 2:21

He himself bore our sins in his body on the tree; so that, having died to sins, we might live for righteousness. By his wounds you have been healed.

1 PETER 2:24

For *Christ also suffered for sins* once for all, *the righteous for the unrighteous, that he might bring you to God.* He was put to death in the flesh but made alive by the Spirit.

1 PETER 3:18

He himself is the atoning sacrifice for our sins, and not only for ours, but also for those of the whole world.

1 JOHN 2:2

This is how we have come to know love: *He laid down his life for us.* We should also lay down our lives for our brothers and sisters.

1 JOHN 3:16

Appendix B:
Glossary

Active Obedience:
Christ's perfect submission and obedience to the Mosaic law and the will of the Father.

Adoption:
An act of God through which He makes us members of His family. It is God's response to our faith and trust in Christ for salvation.

Ascension:
The moment when Jesus rose to heaven in His bodily form. This took place forty days after His resurrection from the dead.

Atonement:
A term referring to how Christ—through His life, death, resurrection, ascension, and return—has conquered sin and all its effects, offered sinners reconciliation to God, and promised to renew all creation.

Calling:
An act of God whereby He speaks through human proclamation of the gospel to summon elect individuals to Himself in such a way that they respond in saving faith.

Consequent Absolute Necessity:
One of two predominant views of God's plan for Jesus's crucifixion; this view suggests that the death of Jesus was the only means by which God could have saved sinners from their sin.

Consequent Hypothetical Necessity:
One of two predominant views of God's plan for Jesus's crucifixion; this view suggests that though God chose to make the death of Jesus the means by which He would save sinners from their sin, hypothetically, He could have chosen a different way to give sinners salvation.

Elect, the:
Those people whom God chose for salvation before the foundation of the world.

Expiation:
To cover or cleanse sin.

Fall, the:
The sin of Adam and Eve in the garden, which introduced sin into the created order.

Glorification:
The final of the three stages of biblical salvation in which we are freed from the presence of sin. It involves the resurrection of the bodies of believers, the subsequent reuniting of their bodies with their souls, and the changing of the bodies of all believers who remain alive to be like the resurrected body of Christ.

Inaugurated Eschatology:
Events in the end times (eschatology) that began (or were inaugurated) with the life, death, and resurrection of Christ.

Intercession:
Jesus's work as the Great High Priest of making petitions before God on behalf of His people.

Justified/Justification:
The first of the three stages of biblical salvation in which believers are freed from the penalty of sin. This is a legal act of God through which He considers our sins forgiven, considers Christ's righteousness as belonging to us, and declares us righteous in His sight.

Limited Atonement:
The view that Christ's death paid for the sins of the elect.

Multi-Intentioned Atonement:
The view that Christ's death paid the penalty for the sins of all people, making it possible for all who believe to be saved. Those who believe are those whom God has ordained.

New Covenant:
The covenant originally promised to God's people in Jeremiah 31 and Ezekiel 36 and inaugurated through the death of Jesus Christ. In the New Covenant, God promises the forgiveness of sin, an intimate relationship with Himself, and an indwelling of the Spirit.

New Jerusalem:
The future dwelling place of God's people in the new heaven and new earth that is described in Revelation 21.

Old Covenant:
The covenant made with Moses and the people of Israel at Mount Sinai; also referred to as the Mosaic covenant.

Passive Obedience:
The sufferings of Christ's life, including His death, in which He paid the penalty for sin.

Propitiation:
The appeasement of God's wrath through the death of Christ.

Purgatory:
Believed to be a place or state of being for those who are in friendship with God but who need purification from their sins in order to enter into heaven. However, the existence of purgatory is not supported by Scripture.

Reconciliation:
The restoration of a relationship. In Christian theology, it refers to the restoration of the relationship between God and man and the removal of enmity.

Redemption:
Christ's work of offering His life as a ransom to free sinners from their bondage to sin and Satan.

Regeneration:
The supernatural work of God upon a spiritually dead person in which God gives them spiritual life, His Spirit, and ultimately eternal life.

Sanctification:
The second of the three stages of biblical salvation in which we are progressively freed from the power of sin. The Holy Spirit works in the lives of believers to bring about holiness in their conduct—putting sin to death and making them more like Christ.

Sanhedrin, the:
The supreme council of Jewish religious leaders who made religious and political decisions for the Jewish people.

Second Advent:
See Second Coming.

Second Coming:
Jesus's yet future bodily return to earth from heaven.

Septuagint:
A Greek translation of the Hebrew Old Testament that was commonly used in the time of Jesus and the early church.

Session (of Christ):
A theological term that refers to the fact that Jesus is currently seated at the right hand of the Father; it is often used in conjunction with the work that Jesus is currently doing.

Son of Man:
A title Jesus often used for Himself that alludes to Daniel 7 and speaks of a divine human who will rule over God's kingdom.

Soul Sleep:
A heretical teaching that suggests immortality is a gift of God given to believers at the future resurrection when Christ returns. This belief posits that a believer sleeps in the grave in a totally unconscious state between the time of their death and their final resurrection.

Substitution/Substitutionary Atonement:
Christ's work of taking the punishment we deserve in our place, satisfying God's wrath and covering our sin with His grace.

Trinitarian:
Refers to the Trinity; the doctrine that describes God as three distinct persons in one—Father, Son, and Holy Spirit—who are all equally God.

Union with Christ:
The permanent and unbreakable relationship believers have with Christ that results in sharing His benefits.

Universalism:
An unbiblical belief that God saves all people regardless of their belief in Jesus Christ.

Unlimited Atonement:
The view that Christ's death paid for the sins of all people.

WHAT IS THE GOSPEL?

hank you for reading and enjoying this book with us! We are abundantly grateful for the Word of God, the instruction we glean from it, and the ever-growing understanding it provides for us of God's character. We are also thankful that Scripture continually points to one thing in innumerable ways: the gospel.

We remember our brokenness when we read about the fall of Adam and Eve in the garden of Eden (Genesis 3), where sin entered into a perfect world and maimed it. We remember the necessity that something innocent must die to pay for our sin when we read about the atoning sacrifices in the Old Testament. We read that we have all sinned and fallen short of the glory of God (Romans 3:23) and that the penalty for our brokenness, the wages of our sin, is death (Romans 6:23). We all need grace and mercy, but most importantly, we all need a Savior.

We consider the goodness of God when we realize that He did not plan to leave us in this dire state. We see His promise to buy us back from the clutches of sin and death in Genesis 3:15. And we see that promise accomplished with Jesus Christ on the cross. Jesus Christ knew no sin yet became sin so that we might become righteous through His sacrifice (2 Corinthians 5:21). Jesus was tempted in every way that we are and lived sinlessly. He was reviled yet still yielded Himself for our sake, that we may have life abundant in Him. Jesus lived the perfect life that we could not live and died the death that we deserved.

The gospel is profound yet simple. There are many mysteries in it that we will never understand this side of heaven, but there is still overwhelming weight to its implications in this life. The gospel tells of our sinfulness and God's goodness and a gracious gift that compels a response. We are saved by grace through faith, which means that we rest with faith in the grace that Jesus Christ displayed on the cross (Ephesians 2:8–9). We cannot save ourselves from our brokenness or do any amount of good works to merit God's favor. Still, we can have faith that what Jesus accomplished in His death, burial, and resurrection was more than enough for our salvation and our eternal delight. When we accept God, we are commanded to die to ourselves and our sinful desires and live a life worthy of the calling we have received (Ephesians 4:1). The gospel compels us to be sanctified, and in so doing, we are conformed to the likeness of Christ Himself. This is hope. This is redemption. This is the gospel.

I will put hostility between you and the woman, and between your offspring and her offspring. He will strike your head, and you will strike his heel.
GENESIS 3:15

For all have sinned and fall short of the glory of God.
ROMANS 3:23

For the wages of sin is death, but the gift of God is eternal life in Christ Jesus our Lord.
ROMANS 6:23

He made the one who did not know sin to be sin for us, so that in him we might become the righteousness of God.

2 CORINTHIANS 5:21

For you are saved by grace through faith, and this is not from yourselves; it is God's gift — not from works, so that no one can boast.

EPHESIANS 2:8–9

Therefore I, the prisoner in the Lord, urge you to walk worthy of the calling you have received, with all humility and gentleness, with patience, bearing with one another in love, making every effort to keep the unity of the Spirit through the bond of peace.

EPHESIANS 4:1–3

WHAT TO READ NEXT

ongratulations on making it to the end of *Why Did Jesus Have to Die? | And 20 Other Questions About Jesus's Death, Resurrection, and Ascension*! We pray this book has encouraged you in your walk with Christ. As you're looking for your next great read, we invite you to check out these titles from The Daily Grace Co.®

Faith Questions | Is the Bible Trustworthy?

Do you have questions about God's Word? Perhaps you wonder how we can trust the accuracy of the biblical books, who wrote them, and who decided which books should be included. If you've ever wrestled with any of these big questions, you are not alone—and we've created a resource just for you! *Faith Questions | Is the Bible Trustworthy?* is designed to answer your biggest questions about the Bible in a clear, easily understandable way. (For answers to even more questions, check out the other books in our *Faith Questions* series, covering topics like purpose, suffering, and truth.)

The Bible Study Handbook | ***A Comprehensive Guide to Reading, Understanding, and Applying the Bible***

We know how challenging it can be to understand the Bible and how intimidating it can feel to study Scripture. Yet at the same time, we know how important Bible study is to spiritual growth! That is why The Daily Grace Co.® team created *The Bible Study Handbook*! Whether you are new to studying the Bible or a regular reader of God's Word, *The Bible Study Handbook* is the tool you need to help you grow in your study of Scripture and take your knowledge of the Bible to the next level.

The Prayer Handbook | ***A Comprehensive Guide to the Practice of Prayer***

Like Bible study, prayer is a powerful discipline for spiritual growth—and more than that, it's a gift to commune with our Creator through prayer! However, many believers feel unconfident, inconsistent, or even unsure when it comes to how to practically form a practice of prayer in their everyday lives. Enter *The Prayer Handbook*, a comprehensive guide designed to teach you what Scripture says about prayer and how you can develop a confident, consistent, and joyful practice of prayer in your everyday life. Whether you are new to prayer or have been praying for years, *The Prayer Handbook* is for you!

Find these titles—and more resources to help you know and love God and His Word— at www.thedailygraceco.com. Happy reading!

BIBLIOGRAPHY

Aland, Kurt, Matthew Black, Carlo M. Martini, Bruce M. Metzger, Maurice A. Robinson, and Allen Wikgren. *The Greek New Testament, Fourth Revised Edition (with Morphology)*. Deutsche Bibelgesellschaft, 2006.

Allberry, Sam. *What God Has to Say about Our Bodies: How the Gospel Is Good News for Our Physical Selves*. Crossway. 2021.

Barry, John D., ed. *The Lexham Bible Dictionary*. Lexham Press, 2016.

Bass, Justin W. *The Bedrock of Christianity: The Unalterable Facts of Jesus' Death and Resurrection*. Lexham Press, 2020.

Bauer, Walter, and Frederick William Danker. *A Greek-English Lexicon of the New Testament and Other Early Christian Literature*. 3rd ed. University of Chicago Press, 2000.

Berkhof, Louis. *Systematic Theology*. Combined ed. William B. Eerdmans Publishing Co., 1996.

Berkhof, Louis. *Systematic Theology*. William B. Eerdmans Publishing Company, 1994.

Bird, Michael F. *Evangelical Theology: A Biblical and Systematic Introduction*. Zondervan Academic, 2013.

Bonhoeffer, Dietrich. *The Cost of Discipleship*. Simon & Schuster, Inc., 1995.

Bridges, Jerry. "The Resurrection of Jesus." *Ligonier*. December 19, 2008. https://learn.ligonier.org/devotionals/resurrection-jesus.

Calvin, John. *Calvin: Institutes of the Christian Religion.* Edited by John T. McNeill. Translated by Ford Lewis Battles. Vol. 2. Westminster John Knox Press, 2011.

Carson, D. A., ed. *NIV Biblical Theology Study Bible.* Zondervan, 2018.

Carson, D. A. *The Gospel according to John,* The Pillar New Testament Commentary. William B. Eerdemans Publishing Company, 1991.

Chaffey, Tim. "Christ's Resurrection—Four Accounts, One Reality." *Answers in Genesis.* April 5, 2015. https://answersingenesis.org/jesus/resurrection/christs-resurrection-four-accounts-one-reality/?srsltid=AfmBOoojp2wIEz-6V4jvVrjS7chgbIJtmt4gNrpNn1T6TnrtFMVQrNfQg.

Demarest, Bruce. *The Cross and Salvation: The Doctrine of Salvation.* Crossway, 1997.

Dennis, Lane T., and Wayne Grudem, eds. *The ESV Study Bible.* Crossway, 2008.

DeRouchie, Jason S. "The Day of the Lord." *The Gospel Coalition.* Accessed January 19, 2025. https://www.thegospelcoalition.org/essay/the-day-of-the-lord/.

DeYoung, Kevin. "How Does Christ's Resurrection Benefit Us?" *The Gospel Coalition.* May 26, 2009. https://www.thegospelcoalition.org/blogs/kev-in-deyoung/how-does-christs-resurrection-benefit/.

Dieter, Melvin E., Anthony A. Hoekema, Stanley M. Horton, J. Robertson McQuilkin, and John F. Walvoord. *Five Views on Sanctification.* Edited by Stanley N. Gundry. Zondervan, 1987.

Drimalla, Shara, and BibleProject Team. "Why Does the Ascension of Jesus Matter?" *Bible Project.* December 9, 2021. https://bibleproject.com/articles/the-ascension-of-jesus/.

Duncan, Ligon. "Propitiation." *The Gospel Coalition.* Accessed December 30, 2024. https://www.thegospelcoalition.org/essay/propitiation/.

Enns, Paul. *The Moody Handbook of Theology Revised and Expanded.* Moody Publishers, 2014.

Eveson, Philip. "The Doctrine of Justification." *The Gospel Coalition.* Accessed December 11, 2024. https://www.thegospelcoalition.org/essay/the-doc-trine-of-justification/.

Flavius Josephus. "The Antiquities of the Jews." *The Works of Josephus.* Translated by William Whiston. Hendrickson Publishers, 1987. https://www.pbs.org/wgbh/pages/frontline/shows/religion/maps/primary/josephusjesus.html.

France, R. T. *The Gospel of Matthew.* New International Commentary on the Old and New Testament. William B. Eerdmans Publishing Company, 2007.

Gaius Suetonius Tranquillus. "The Life of Claudius." *The Lives of the Twelve Caesars.* The Loeb Classical Library. 1914. https://penelope.uchicago.edu/Thayer/E/Roman/Texts/Suetonius/12Caesars/Claudius*.html#note75.

Gardoski, Ken. "The Will of God and the Death of Christ: A Case for the Universal Scope of the Atonement." *Journal of Ministry and Theology* 15:1 (2011). https://www.galaxie.com/article/jmat15-1-03.

Gerwig, Greta, dir. *Barbie.* Warner Brothers, 2023.

Got Questions Ministries. *Got Questions? Bible Questions Answered.* Logos Bible Software, 2002–2013.

Green, Michael. *The Message of Matthew: The Kingdom of Heaven.* The Bible Speaks Today. InterVarsity Press, 2001.

Grenz, Stanley J. *Theology for the Community of God.* William B. Eerdmans Publishing Company, 2000.

Grudem, Wayne A. *Systematic Theology: An Introduction to Biblical Doctrine.* Zondervan Academic, 2020.

Hendriksen, William. *New Testament Commentary: Matthew.* Baker Book House, 1973.

Hodge, A. A. *The Atonement.* Presbyterian Board of Publication, 1867.

Horton, Michael. *Pilgrim Theology: Core Doctrines for Christian Disciples.* Zondervan Academic, 2012.

IMDbPro. "2023 Worldwide Box Office." *Box Office Mojo.* Accessed March 11, 2025. https://www.boxofficemojo.com/year/world/2023/.

Johnson, Raymond. "Matthew 27:51–54 Revisited: A Narratological Re-Appropriation." *The Southern Baptist Journal of Theology,* 18, no. 4 (2014): 31–50.

Jones, David A. *Old Testament Quotations and Allusions in the New Testament.* Logos Bible Software, 2009.

Keener, Craig S. *Matthew*. Vol. 1. of The IVP New Testament Commentary Series. InterVarsity Press, 1997.

Keller, Timothy. *The Meaning of Marriage: Facing the Complexities of Commitment with the Wisdom of God*. Dutton, 2011.

Letham, Robert. *Systematic Theology*. 2nd ed. Crossway, 2017.

Letham, Robert. "The Ascension of Christ." *The Gospel Coalition*. Accessed December 29, 2024. https://www.thegospelcoalition.org/essay/ascension-of-christ/.

Lethem, Robert. "10 Things You Should Know about Inaugurated Eschatology." *Crossway*. November 21, 2019. https://www.crossway.org/articles/10-things-you-should-know-about-inaugurated-eschatology/.

Liguori, Ryan. "Why Don't the Gospels Match?" *N.T. Wright Online*. Accessed January 26, 2025. https://www.ntwrightonline.org/why-dont-the-gospels-match/.

Luyken, Jan. Hemelvaart van Christus. 1712. Etching, height 118 mm x width 154 mm. Rijksmuseum, Amsterdam. RP-P-OB-46.074. https://id.rijksmuseum.nl/200227381.

Luyken, Jan. Kruisiging van Christus. 1712. Etching, height 118 mm x width 154 mm. Rijksmuseum, Amsterdam. RP-P-OB-46.066. https://id.rijksmuseum.nl/200227374.

Luyken, Jan. Kruisiging van I. Christus. 1681. Etching, height 123 mm x width 77 mm. Rijksmuseum, Amsterdam. RP-P-1896-A-19368-151. https://id.rijksmuseum.nl/200222346.

Luyken, Jan. Opstanding van Christus. 1712. Etching, height 118 mm x width 152 mm. Rijksmuseum, Amsterdam. RP-P-OB-46.068. https://id.rijksmuseum.nl/200227376.

MacArthur, John F. *The MacArthur New Testament Commentary: Matthew 24–28*. Moody Press, 1989.

Mangum, Douglas, ed. *Lexham Context Commentary: New Testament*. Lexham Press, 2020.

Manser, Martin H. *Dictionary of Bible Themes: The Accessible and Comprehensive Tool for Topical Studies*. Martin Manser, 2009.

Merriam-Webster.com Dictionary, s.v. "Propitiate." Accessed March 14, 2025. https://www.merriam-webster.com/dictionary/propitiate.

Milne, Bruce. *The Message of John: Here Is Your King!* The Bible Speaks Today. Inter-Varsity Press, 1993.

Mohler Jr., R. Albert. *The Apostles' Creed: Discovering Authentic Christianity in an Age of Counterfeits.* Nelson Books, 2019.

Morris, Leon. *Luke: An Introduction and Commentary.* Vol. 3 of Tyndale New Testament Commentaries. InterVarsity Press, 1988.

Murray, John. *Redemption Accomplished and Applied.* William B. Eerdmans Publishing Company, 1955.

Murray, John. *Redemption Accomplished and Applied.* William B. Eerdmans Publishing Company, 1955. Reprint, William B. Eerdmans Publishing Company, 2015.

Orr, Peter C. *Exalted above the Heavens: The Risen and Ascended Christ.* New Studies in Biblical Theology. InterVarsity Press, 2018.

Osborne, Grant R. *Zondervan Exegetical Commentary on the New Testament: Matthew.* Zondervan, 2010.

Papa, Matt, Matt Boswell, Bryan Christopher Fowler, Kristyn Getty, and Keith Getty. "Christus Victor (Amen)." *Capitol CMG Publishing.* 2024.

Pate, C. Marvin. *40 Questions About the Historical Jesus.* Kregel, Inc, 2015.

Perman, Matt. "Historical Evidence for the Resurrection." *Desiring God.* September 12, 2007. https://www.desiringgod.org/articles/historical-evidence-for-the-resurrection.

Perry, Tobin. "When Did Jesus Die? (Do We Know the Day and Time?)" *Logos.* March 24, 2023. https://www.logos.com/grow/nook-when-did-jesus-die/.

Pfeiffer, Charles F., Howard F. Vos, and John Rea, eds. *Wycliffe Bible Encyclopedia.* Moody Press, 1975.

Piper, John. "The Present Power of Christ Crucified." Sermon. February 7, 1988. MP3 audio. 35:13. https://www.desiringgod.org/messages/the-present-power-of-christ-crucified.

Pliny the Younger. *The Letters of Pliny the Younger.* Book 10, Letters 1–60. Translated by J. B. Firth. 1900. https://www.attalus.org/old/pliny10b.html.

Powlison, David. *God's Grace in Your Suffering*. Crossway, 2018.

Prior, David. *The Message of 1 Corinthians: Life in the Local Church*. The Bible Speaks Today. InterVarsity Press, 1985.

Rau, Andy. "Questions About Easter: Do the Resurrection Accounts in the Four Gospels Contradict Each Other?" *Bible Gateway*. March 22, 2012. https://www.biblegateway.com/blog/2012/03/questions-about-easter-do-the-resur-rection-accounts-in-the-four-gospels-contradict-each-other/.

Rosner, Brian. "2 Reasons Jesus Died on the Cross." *The Gospel Coalition*. April 10, 2020. https://www.thegospelcoalition.org/article/jesus-died-cross/.

Schaff, Philip. *The Creeds of Christendom: Volumes 1–3*. Delmarva Publications, 2016.

Schnabel, Eckhard J. *Mark*. Tyndale New Testament Commentaries. InterVarsity Press, 2017.

Schreiner, Patrick. *The Ascension of Christ: Recovering a Neglected Doctrine*. Lexham Press, 2020.

Schreiner, Thomas. "Substitutionary Atonement." *The Gospel Coalition*. Accessed December 9, 2024. https://www.thegospelcoalition.org/essay/substitution-ary-atonement/.

Shaw, David M. "The Already and Not-Yet Kingdom." *The Gospel Coalition*. April 8, 2018. https://au.thegospelcoalition.org/article/already-not-yet-kingdom/.

Shenvi, Neil. "4 Points of Evidence for the Resurrection." *Crossway*. March 31, 2023. https://www.crossway.org/articles/4-points-of-evidence-for-the-resur-rection/.

Sinclair, George. "10 Concise Pieces of Evidence for the Resurrection." *The Gospel Coalition*. April 12, 2020. https://ca.thegospelcoalition.org/article/10-con-cise-pieces-of-evidence-for-the-resurrection/.

Sproul, R. C. "Ascension: What Did Jesus Do? - Understanding the Work of Christ with R. C. Sproul." *Ligonier Ministries*. September 2, 2023. YouTube Video. 23:43 https://www.youtube.com/watch?v=yLYeua7bPnI.

Sproul, R. C. "Witnessing His Glory." *Ligonier*. May 15, 2009. https://learn.ligoni-er.org/devotionals/witnessing-his-glory.

Spurgeon, Charles H. "The Three Hours' Darkness: A Sermon Delivered On Lord's Day Morning." No. 1896-32:217. April 18, 1886. At The Metropolitan Tabernacle, Newington.

Treat, Jeremy R. *The Atonement: An Introduction*. Short Studies in Systematic Theology. Edited by Graham A. Cole and Oren R. Martin. Crossway, 2023.

Um, Stephen T. *1 Corinthians: The Word of the Cross*. Preaching the Word. Edited by R. Kent Hughes. Crossway, 2015.

Walls, Jeanette, and Ashley Pearson. "Gibson Makes Act of Contrition in 'Passion.'" *TODAY.com*. January 6, 2004. https://www.today.com/popculture/gibson-makes-act-contrition-passion-wbna3881874.

Ware, Bruce. "Extent of the Atonement: Outline of The Issue, Positions, Key Texts, and Key Theological Arguments." *The Southern Baptist Theological Seminary*. Accessed March 28, 2025. https://www.epm.org/static/uploads/downloads/Extent_of_the_Atonement_by_Bruce_Ware.pdf.

Wenham, G. J., J. A. Motyer, D. A. Carson, and R. T. France. *New Bible Commentary: 21st Century Edition*. Intervarsity Press, 1994.

York, Barry. "Who Killed Jesus?" *Ligonier Ministries*. November 17, 2024. https://learn.ligonier.org/articles/who-killed-jesus.

Youngblood, Ronald F., ed. *Nelson's New Illustrated Bible Dictionary*. Thomas Nelson Publishers, 1995.

The Daily *Grace* Co.®

CONNECT WITH US
@thedailygraceco
@dailygracepodcast

CONTACT US
info@thedailygraceco.com

SHARE
#thedailygraceco

VISIT US ONLINE
www.thedailygraceco.com

MORE DAILY GRACE
Daily Grace® Podcast

We get to experience
Christ crucified,
Christ resurrected, and
Christ ascended.